AF224953

Progressive Patterns For Lefties
Adult Colouring Book

nikk nakk

designs

Progressive Patterns for Lefties - Adult Colouring Book

Copyright 2015 by nikk nakk designs

Created by Niki Palmer and Ros Tulleners

Illustrated by Stuart Campbell, Subrata Dutta, Elshan Gurbanov

First edition 2015
ISBN: 978-1-925422-09-2
www.nikknakkdesigns.com.au

Welcome to the simple pleasure of colouring for left handed adults.

Progressive Patterns for Lefties - Adult Colouring Book has been designed especially for the left handed colorists by our talented creative team who understand the challenges faced by 'lefties' when colouring in conventional books.

Not sure how or where to start? All you really need are some coloured pencils and a good quality pencil sharpener to get started.

Take a chance and use our 'pot luck' method - it is so easy!
Make a up of tea or coffee if you need one.
Find a quiet place to work away from electronic distractions.
Let the book fall open at any page.
Close your eyes and pick up any colour.
Choose a shape and start to colour.
Woohoo ..... You are a colourist!

Soon you will be caught up in your work, your mind will be focused and the realities of the day will drift away. The tension will drain from your body as your pencils reveal the colourful masterpiece under your fingertips. Try to allocate at least 15 -30 minutes a day to this simple, inexpensive way to calm your mind and body.

As your confidence and skill levels grow, you will be ready to experiment with more complex designs, different colouring techniques and begin to explore the amazing range of pencils, crayons, gel and metallic pens chalks and water colour effects - let your imagination run wild, there are no rules.

Most importantly, relax and have fun! The team at nikk nakk designs certainly had fun creating these designs for you to enjoy!

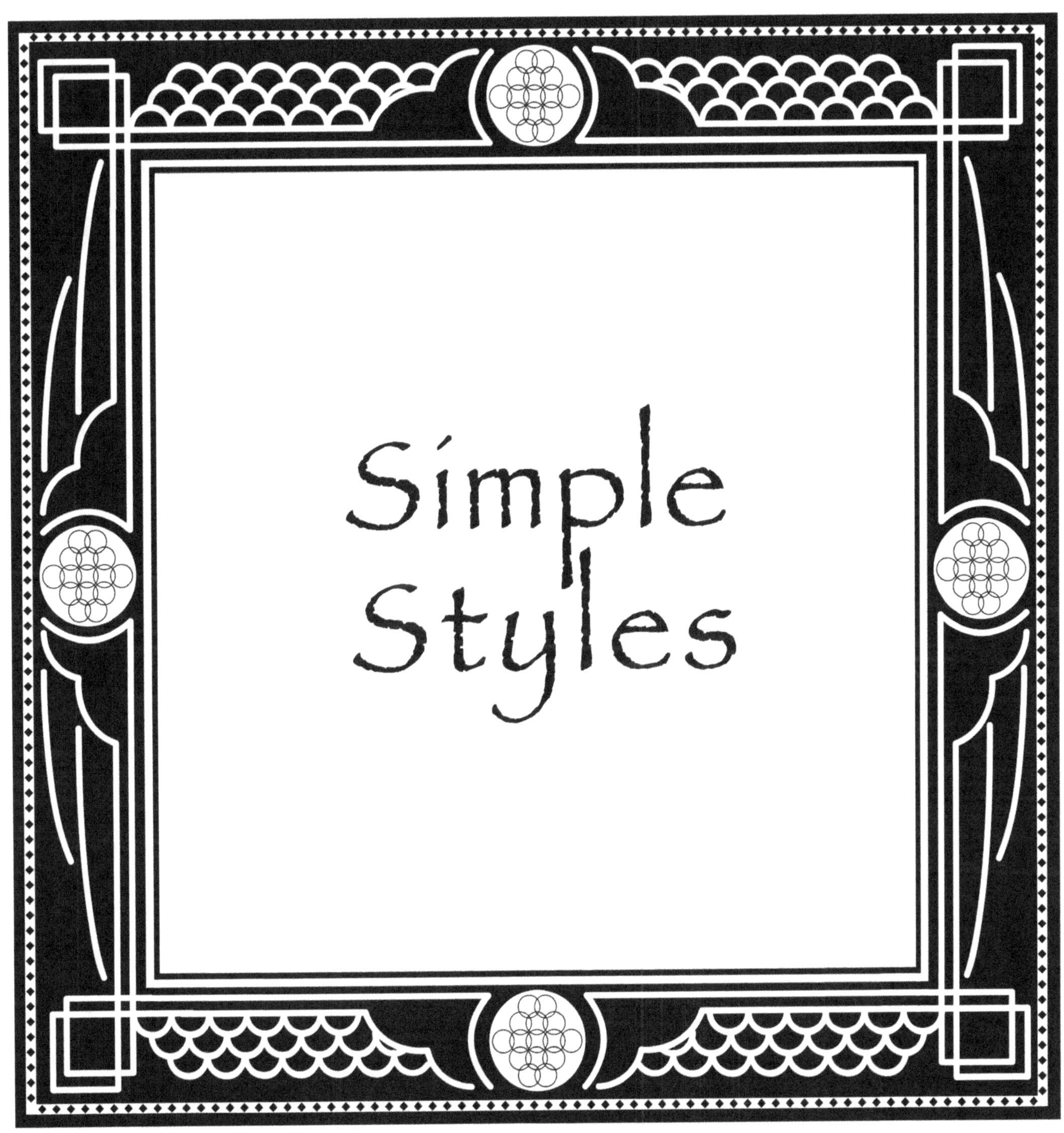
Simple
Styles

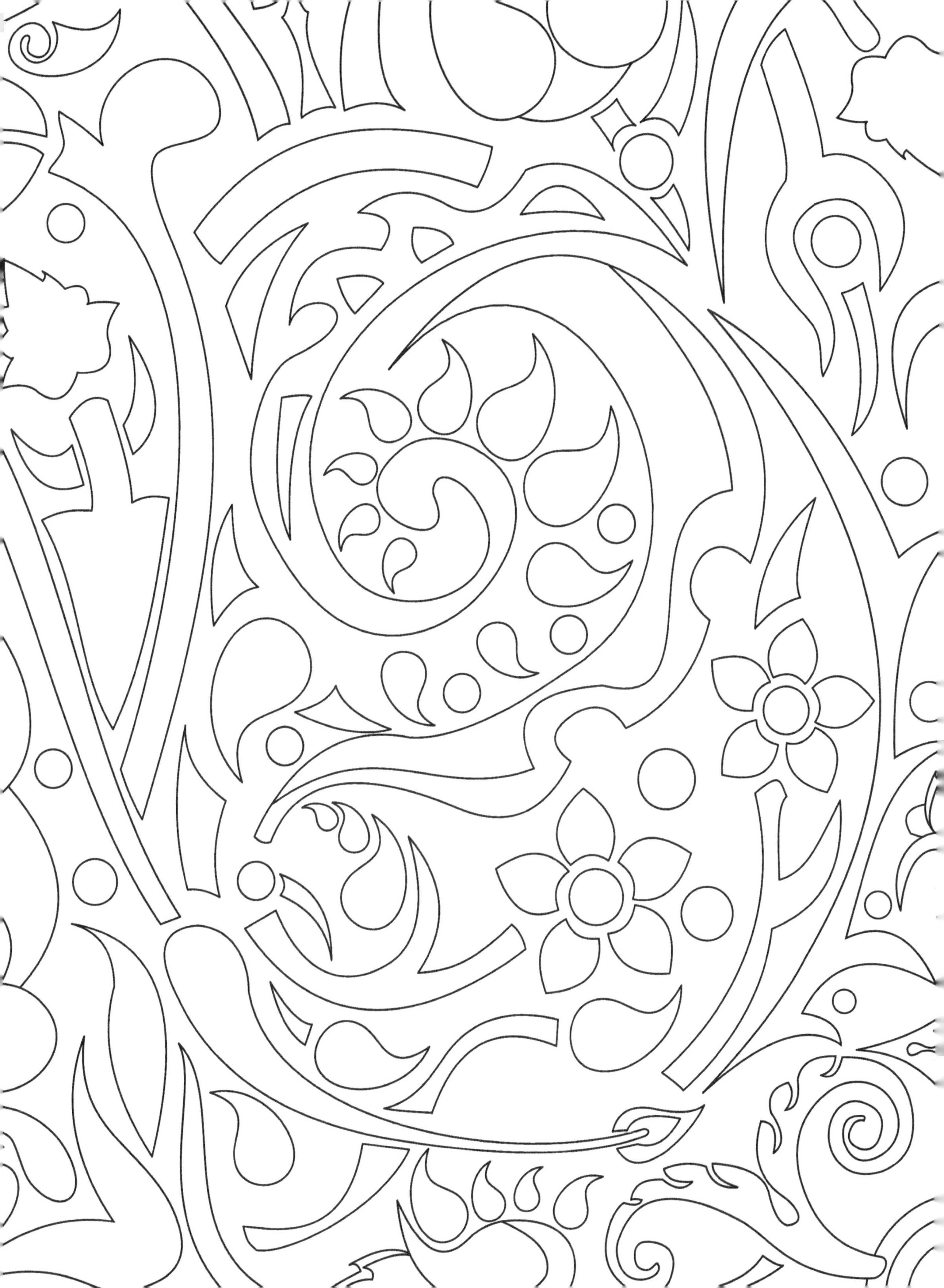

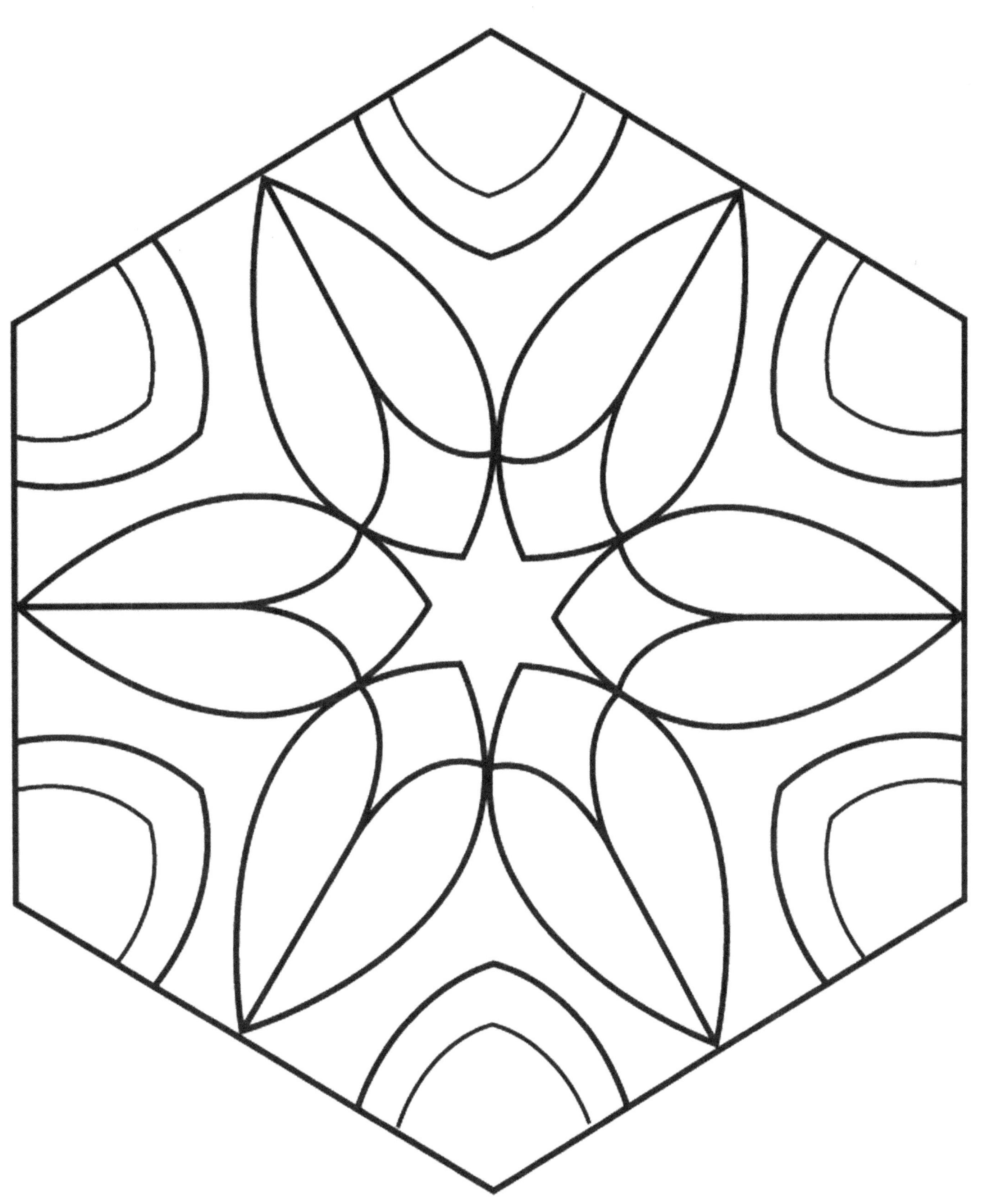

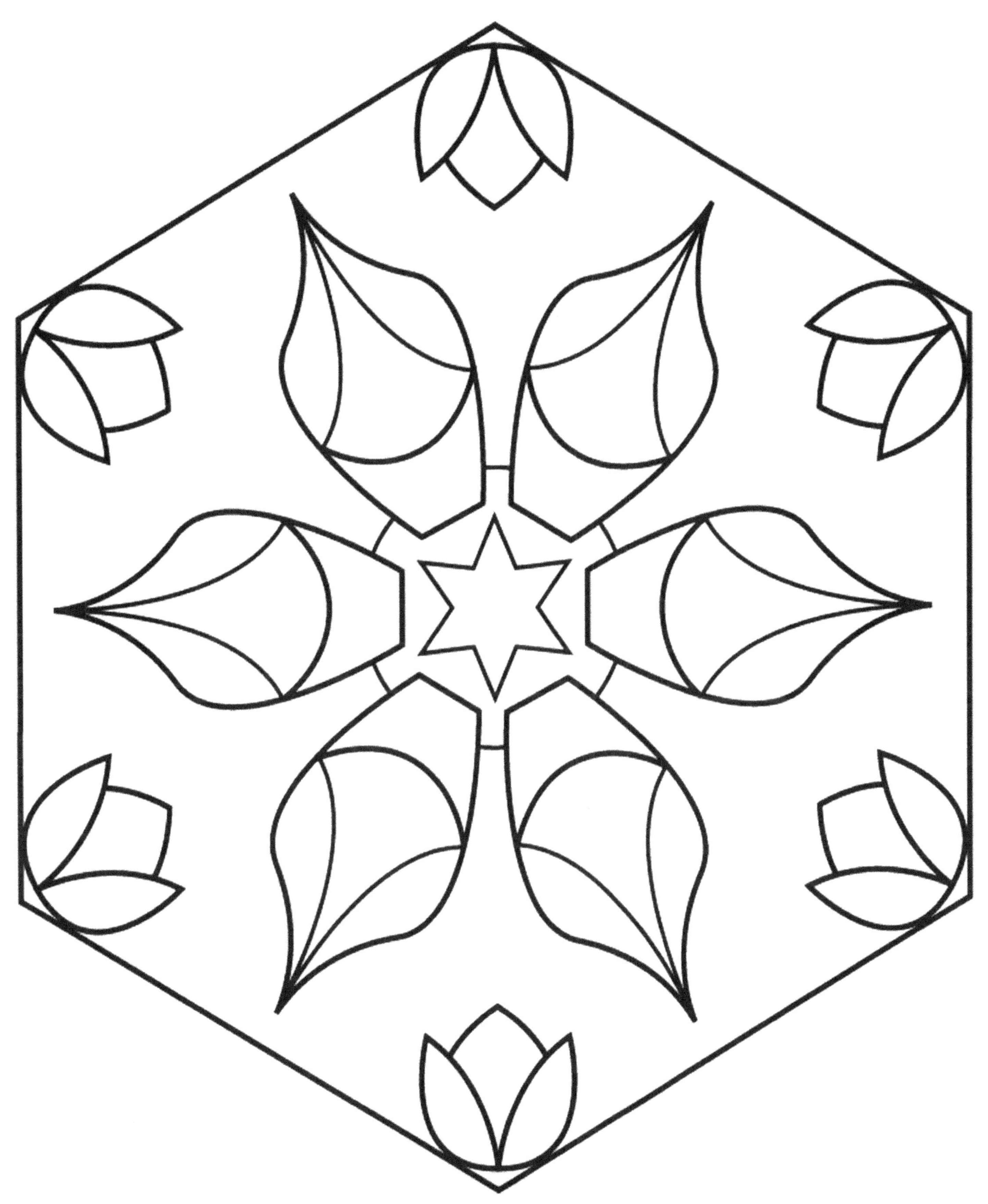

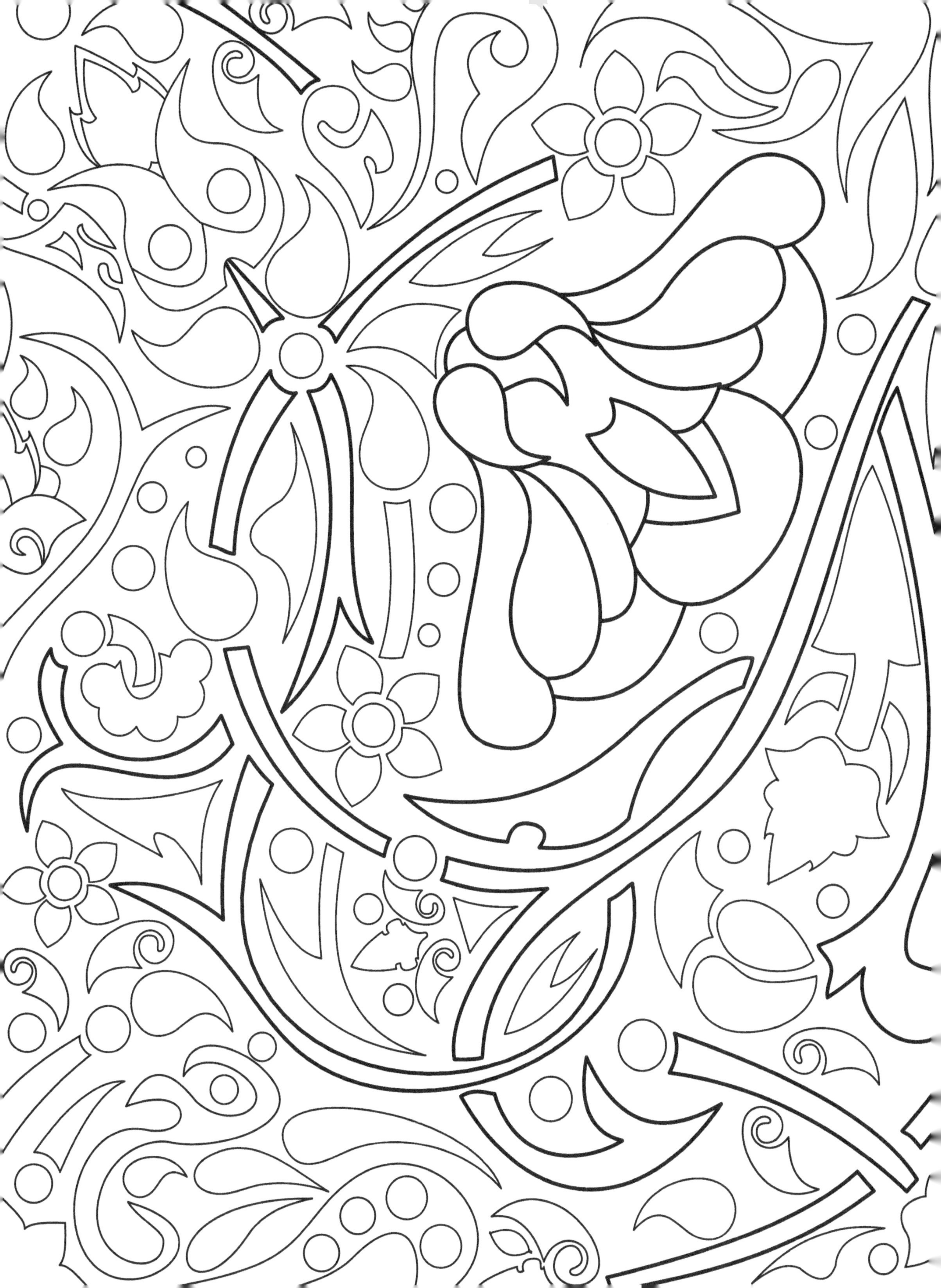

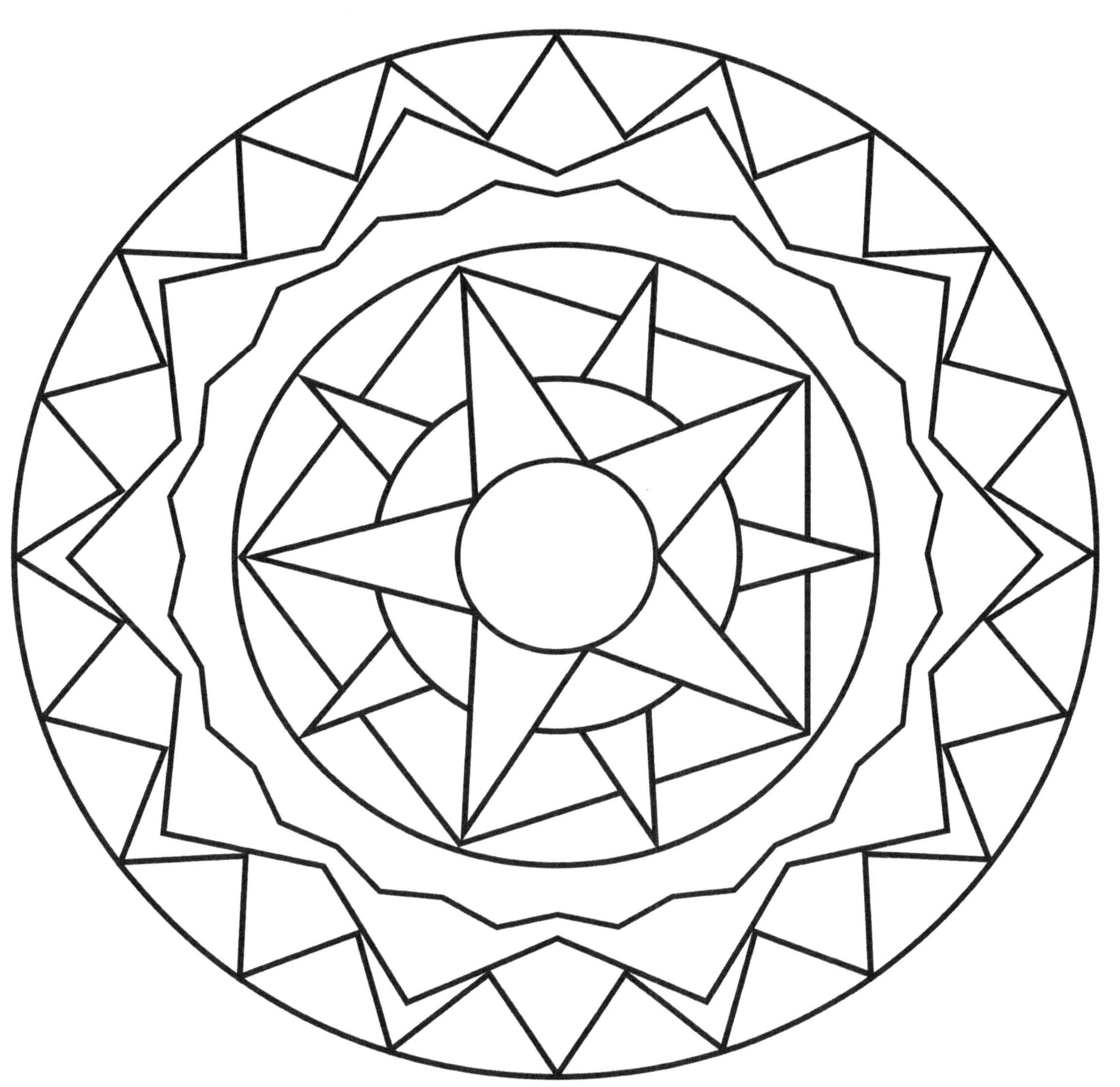

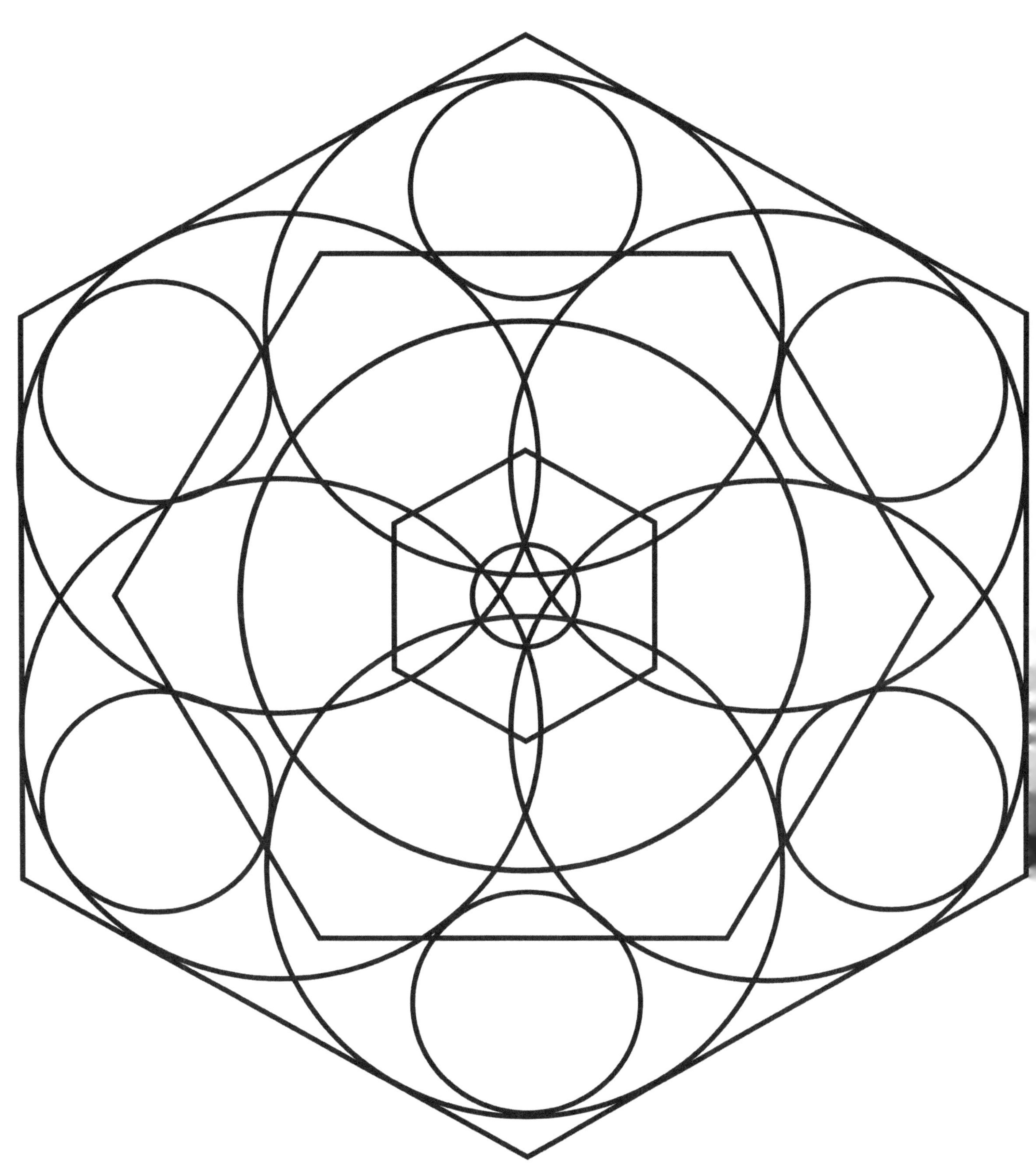

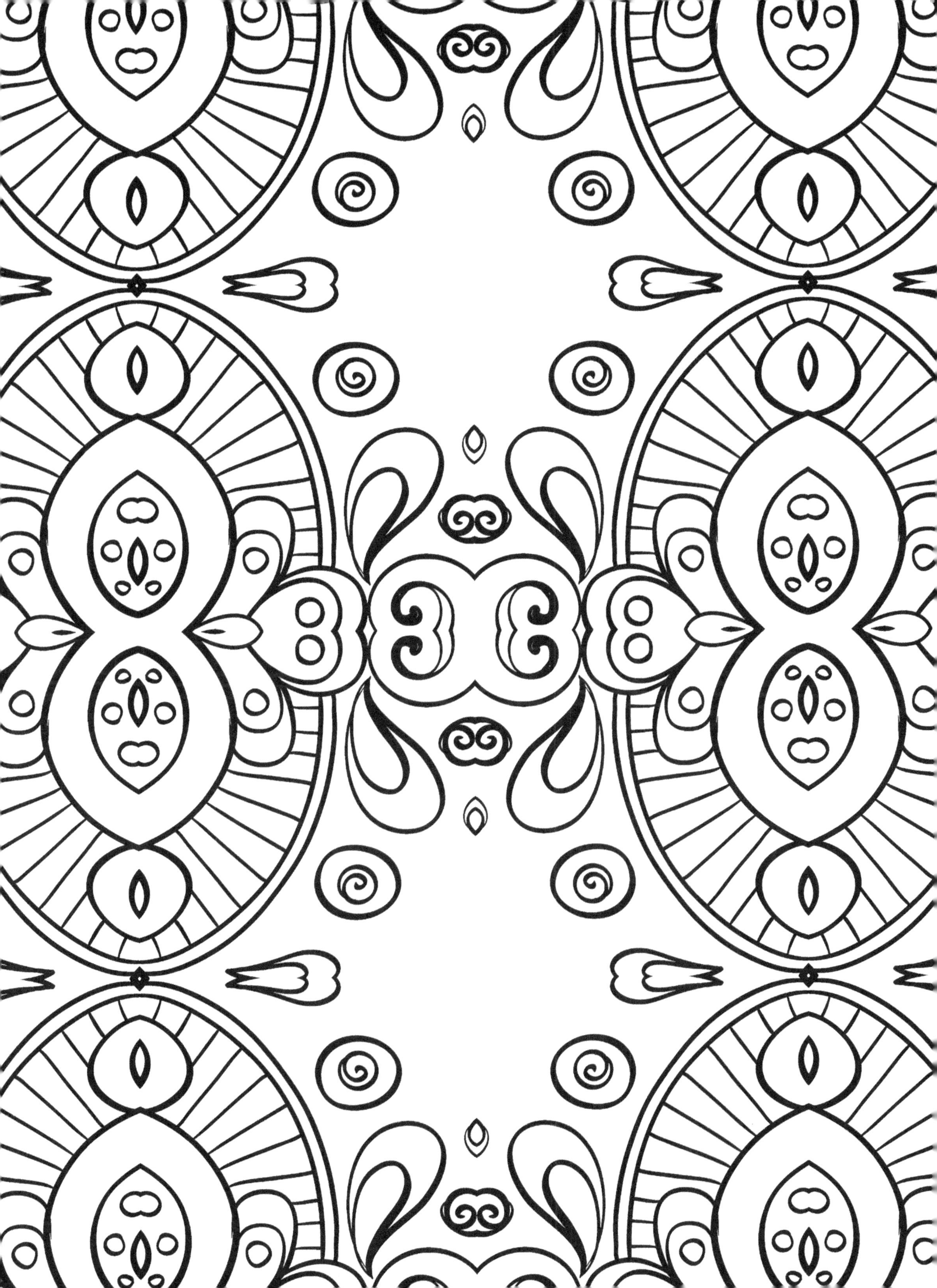

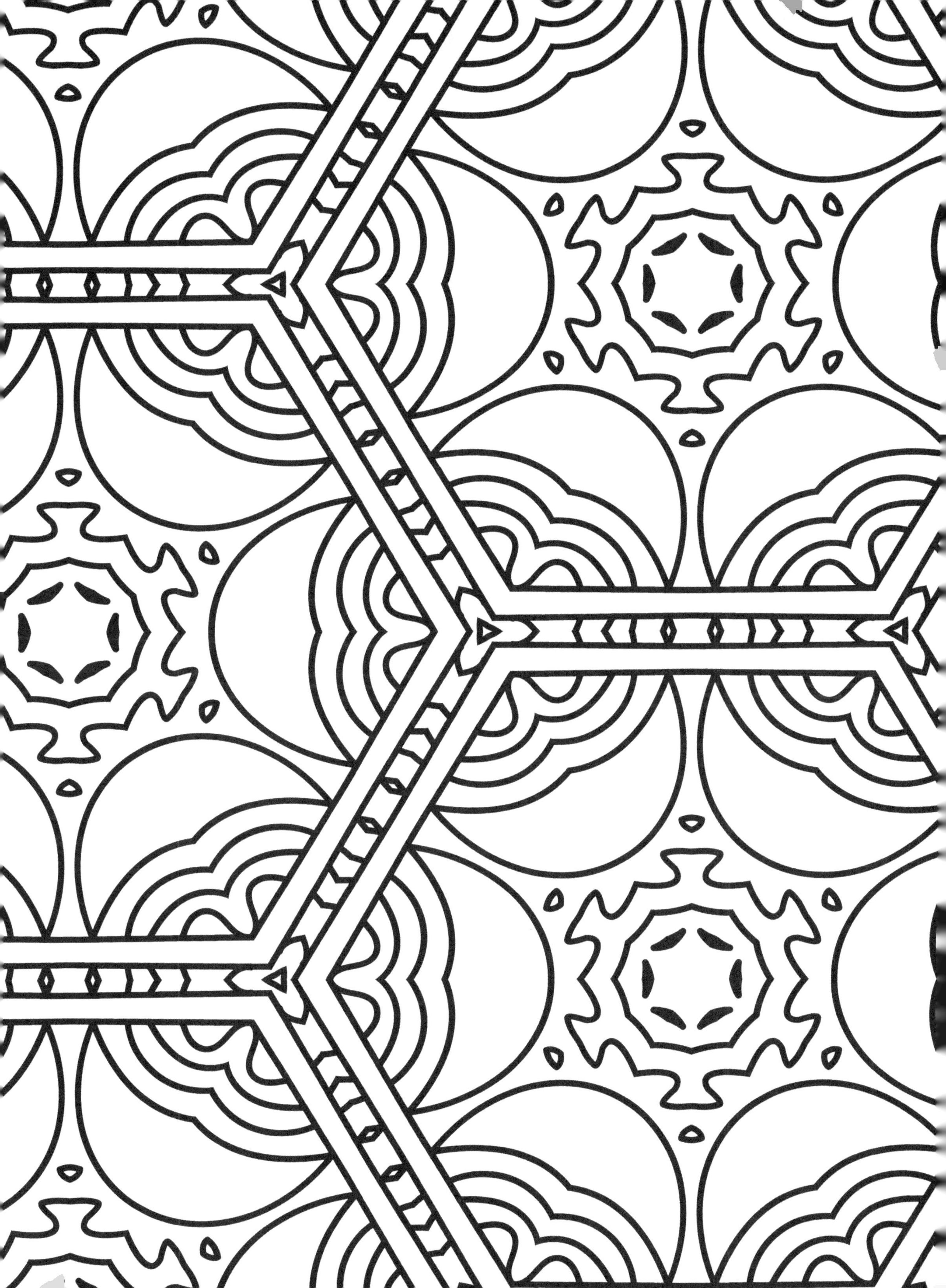

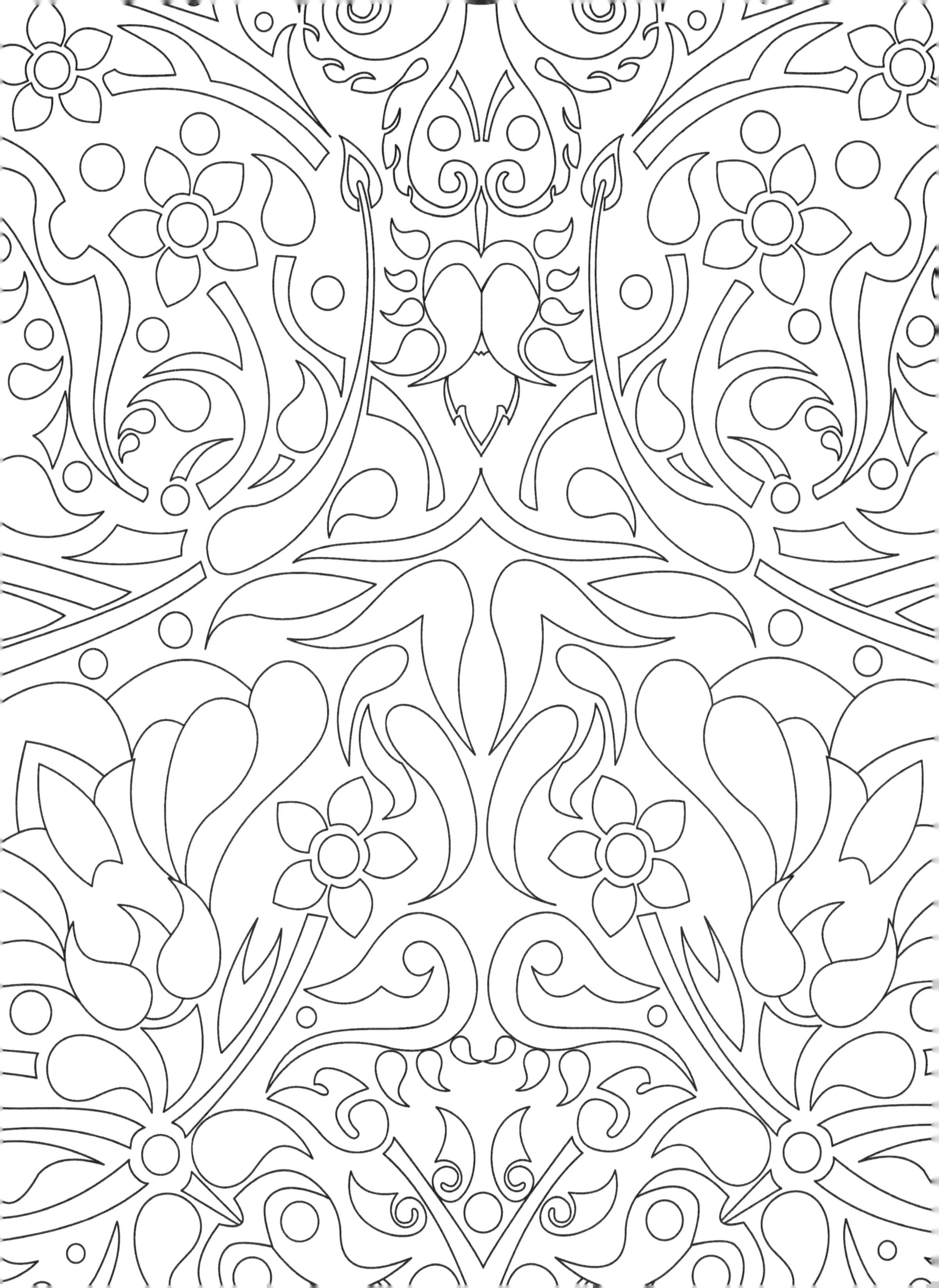

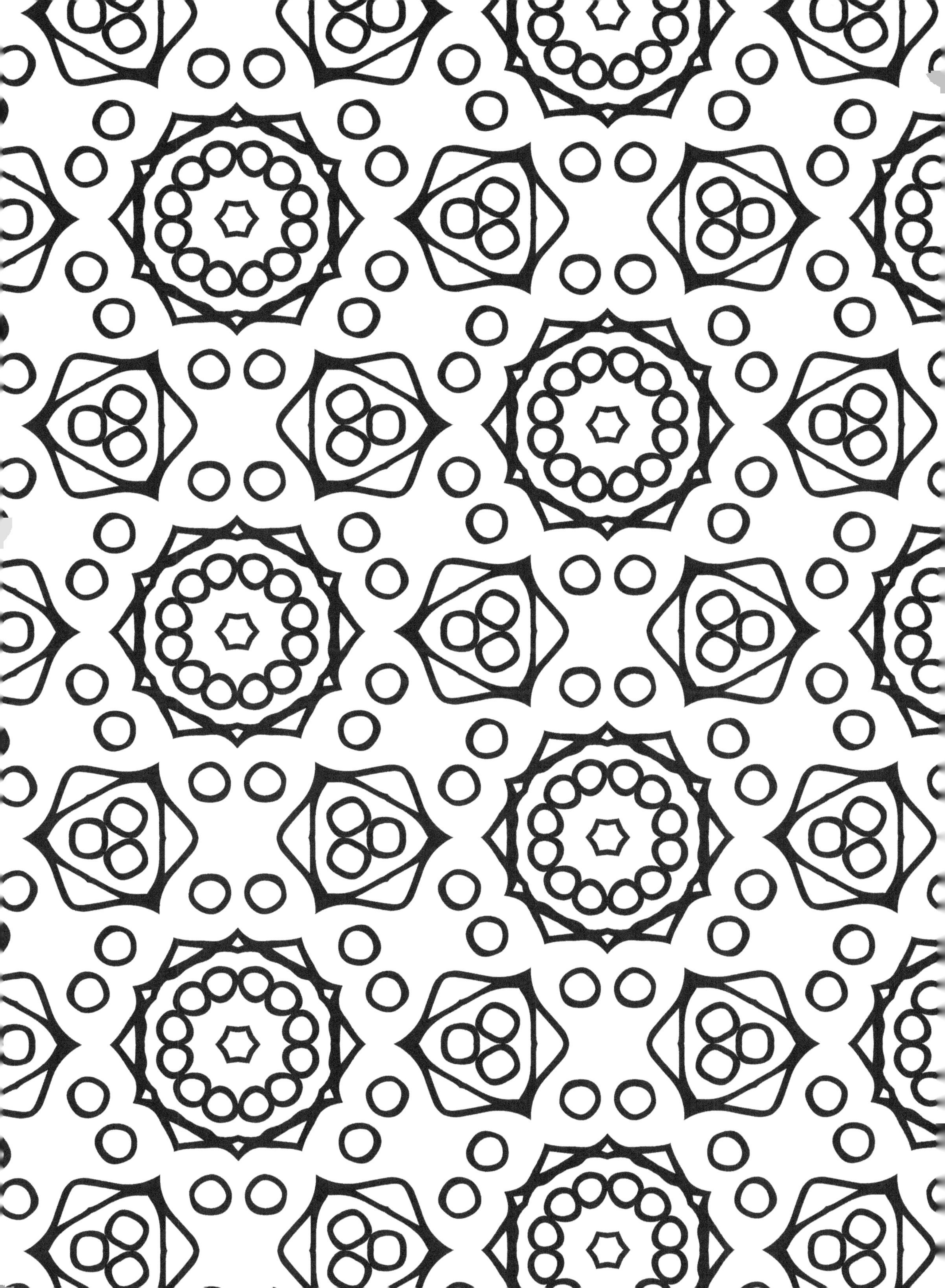

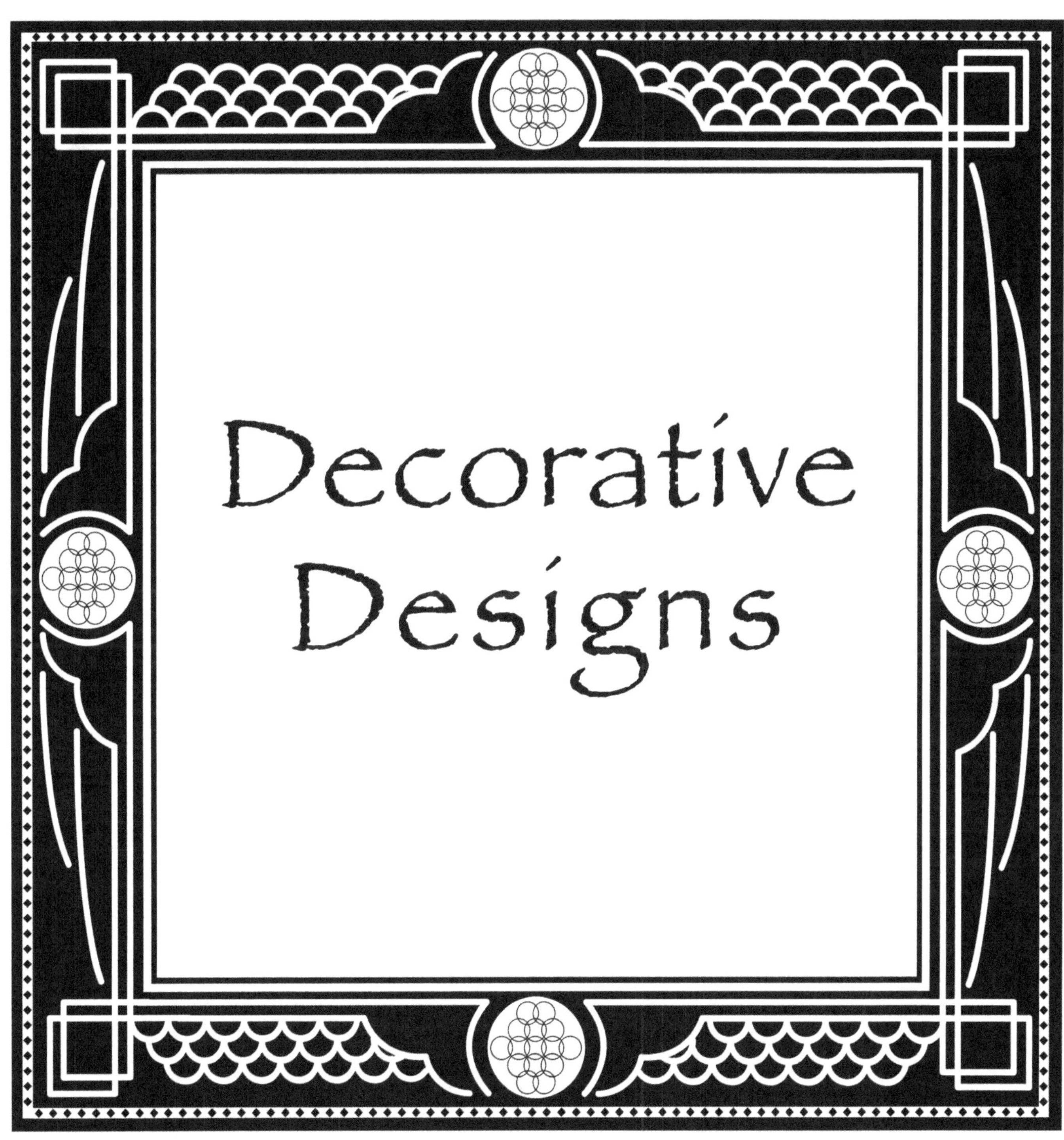

Decorative
Designs

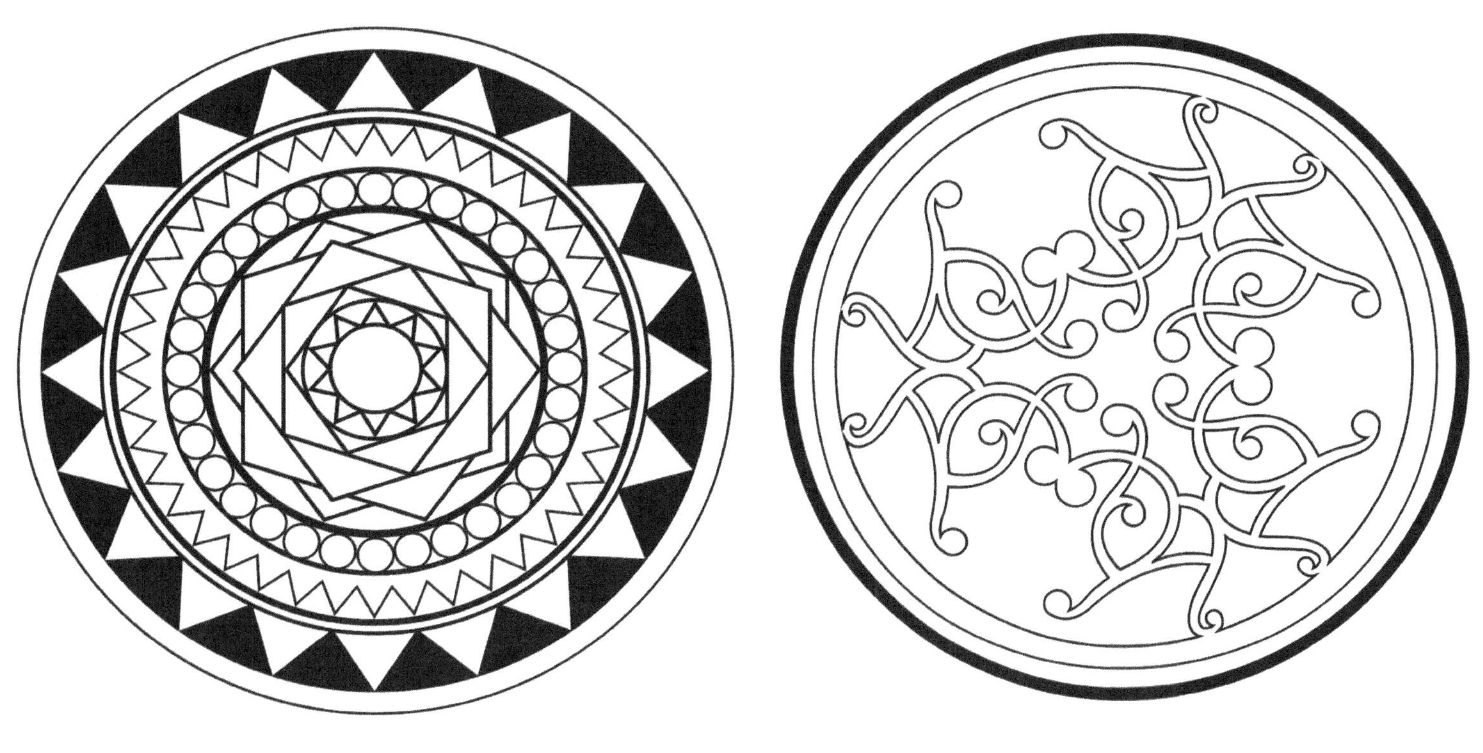

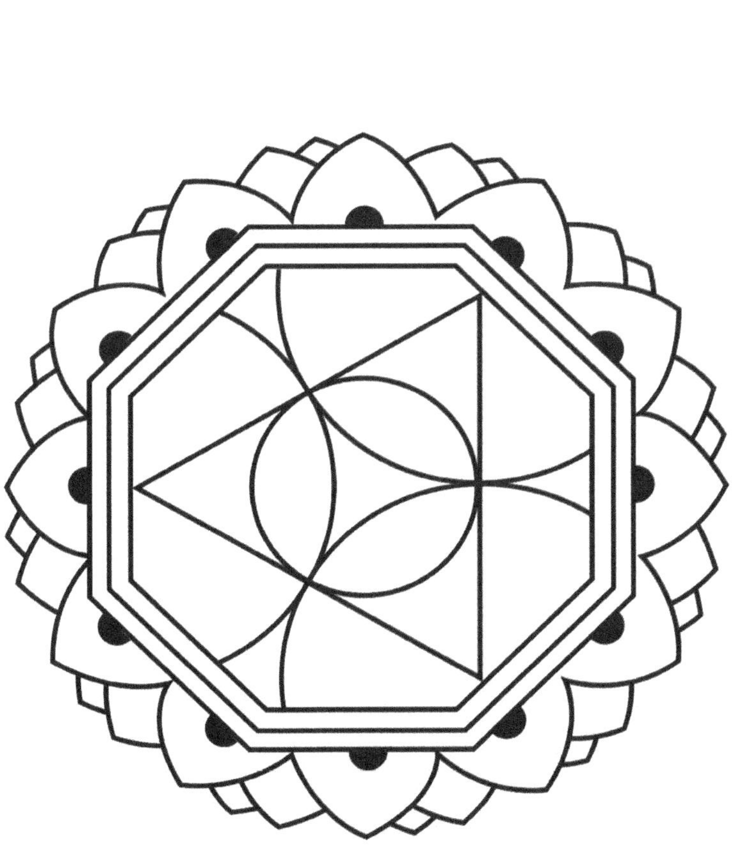

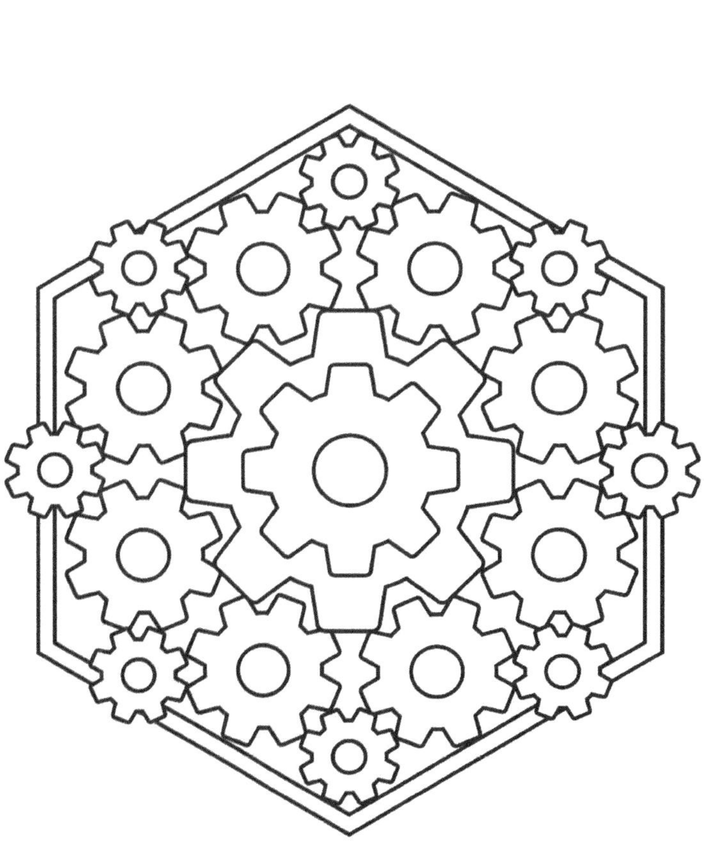

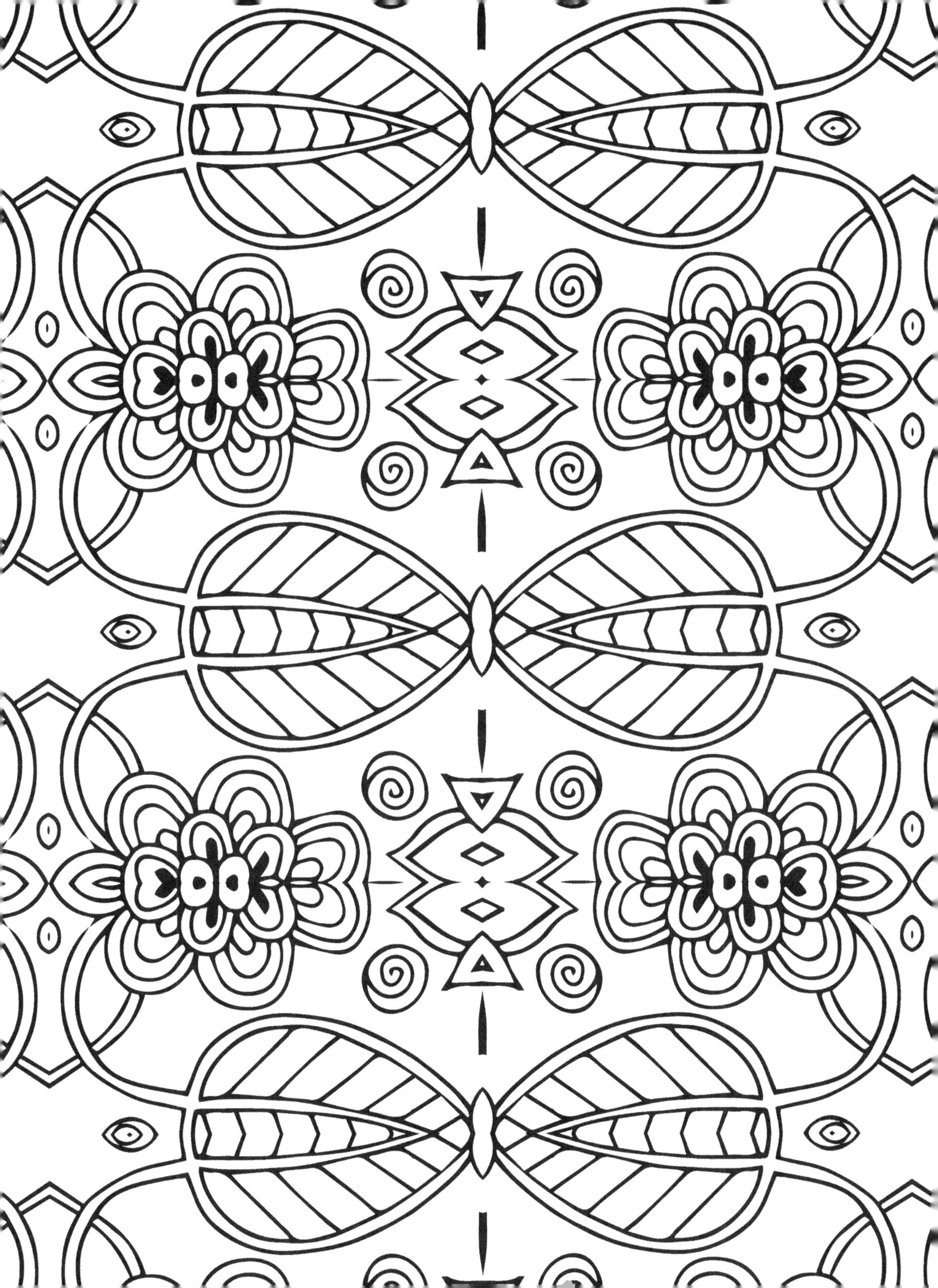

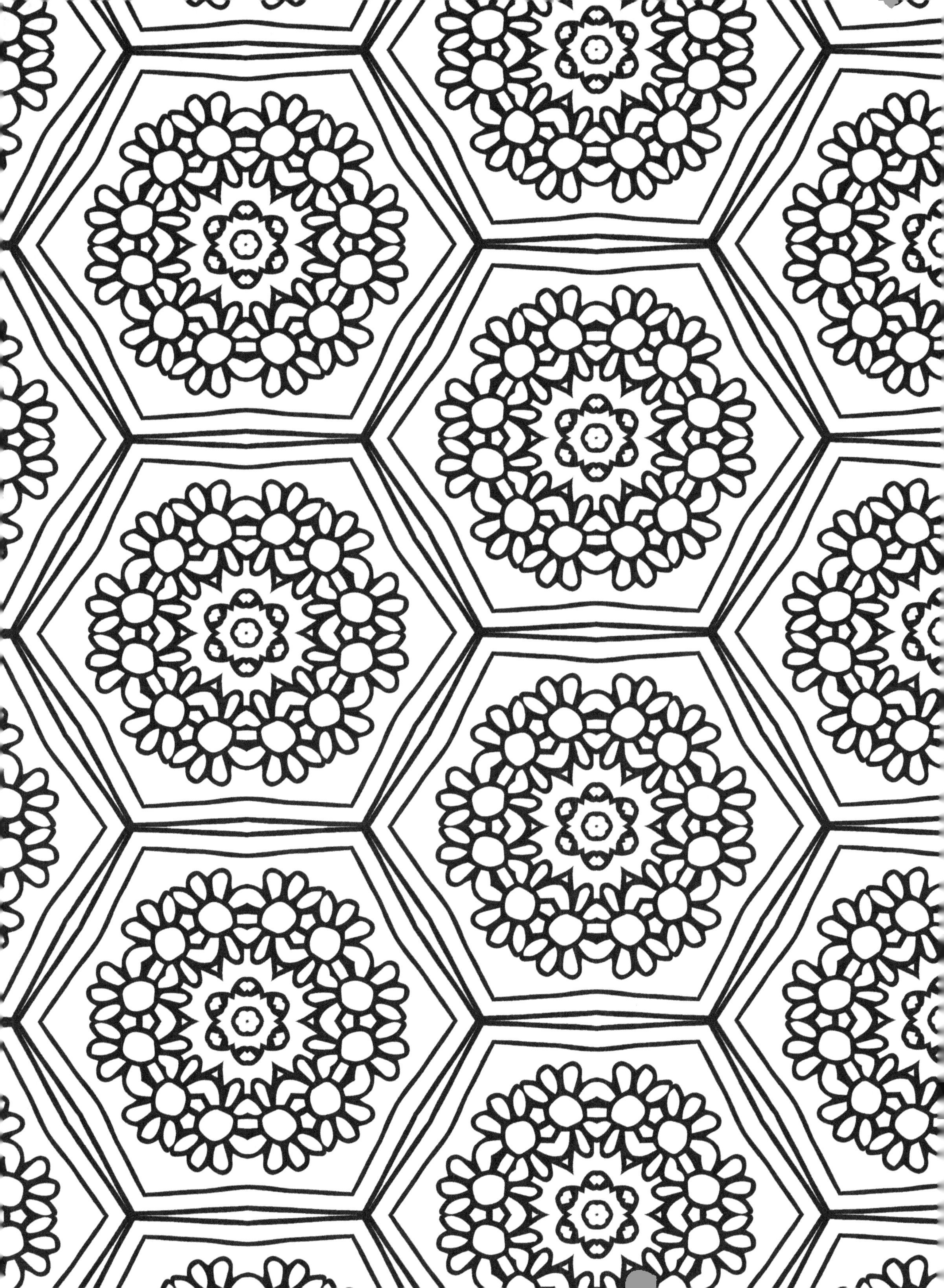

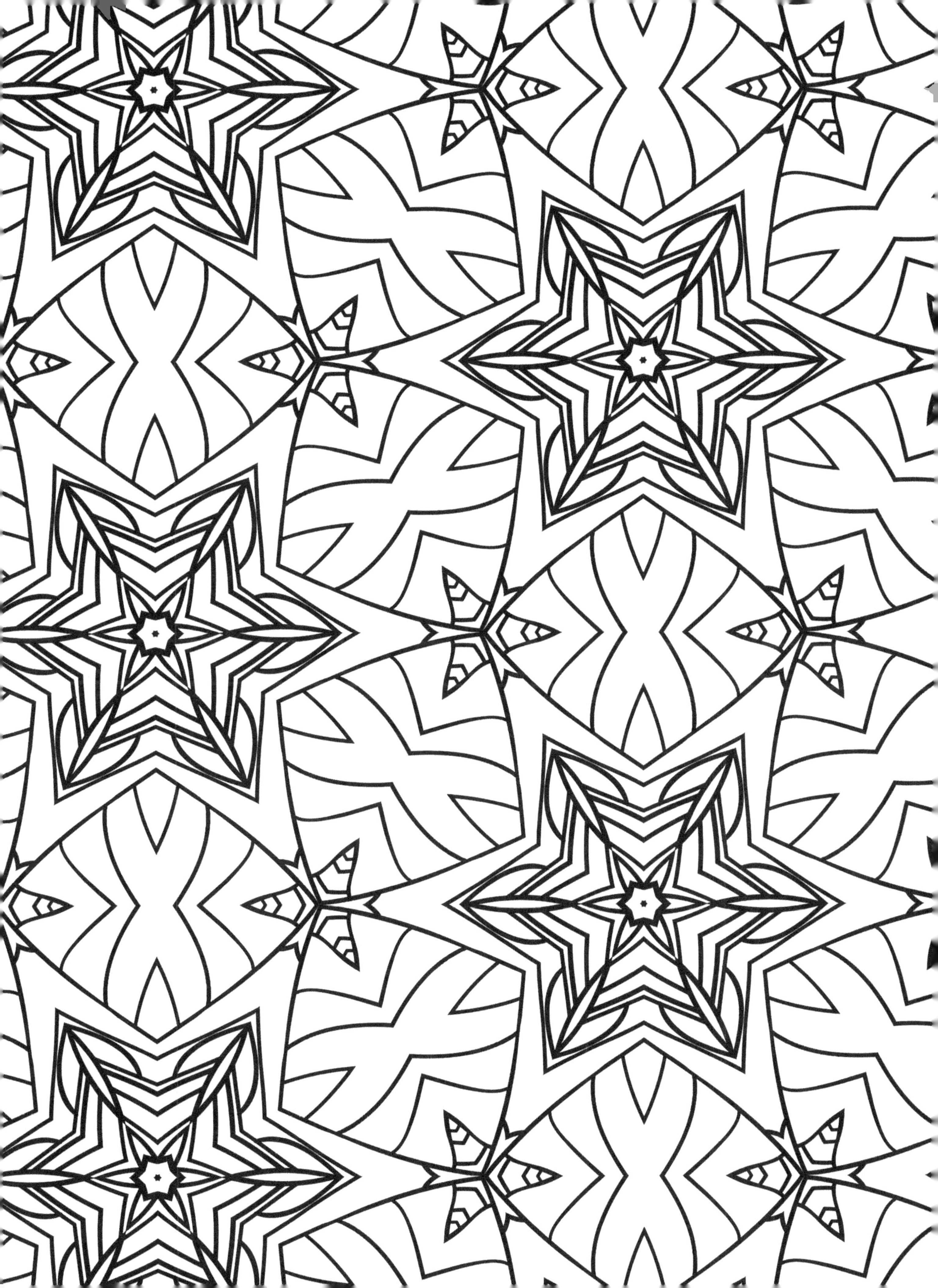

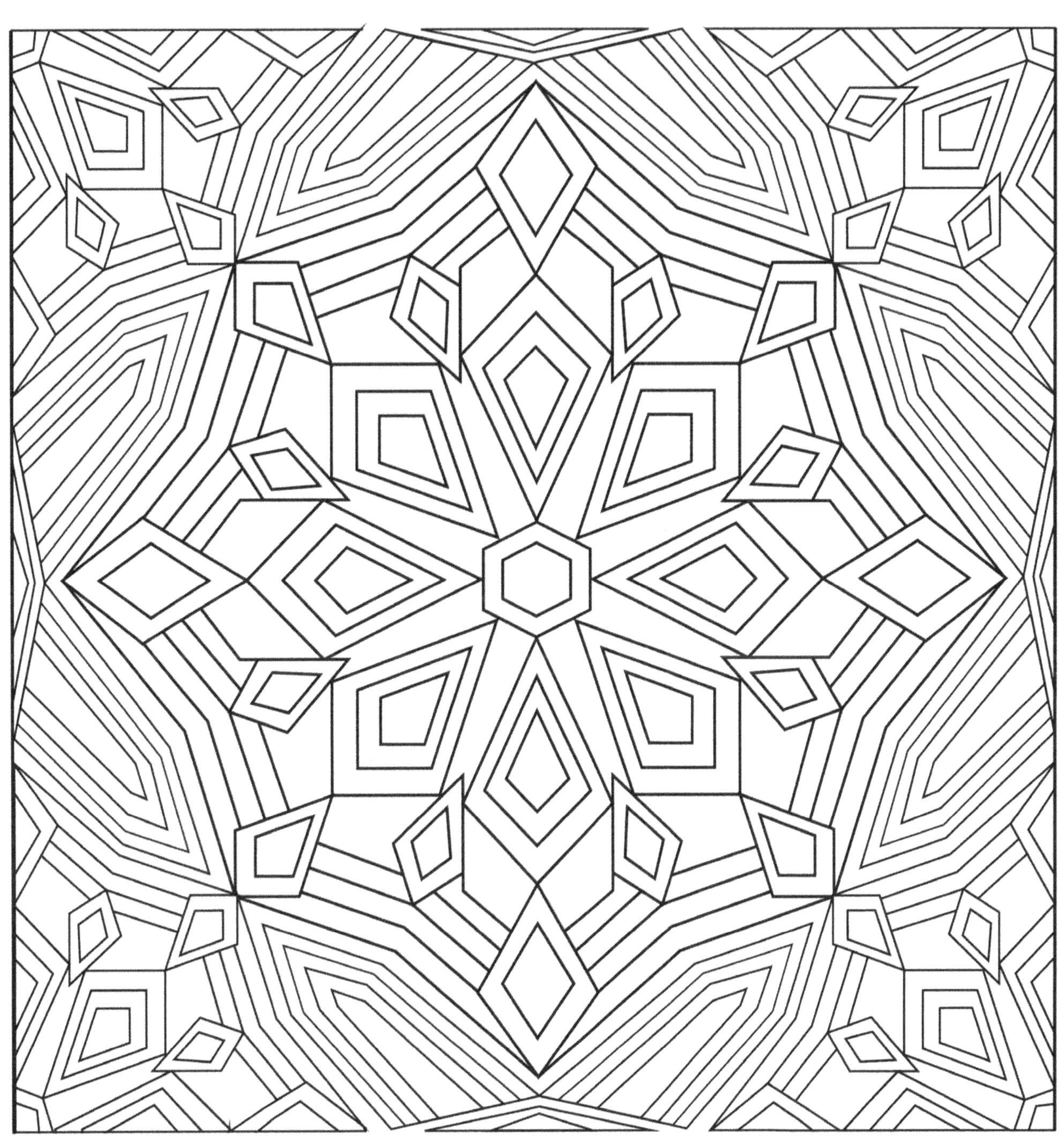

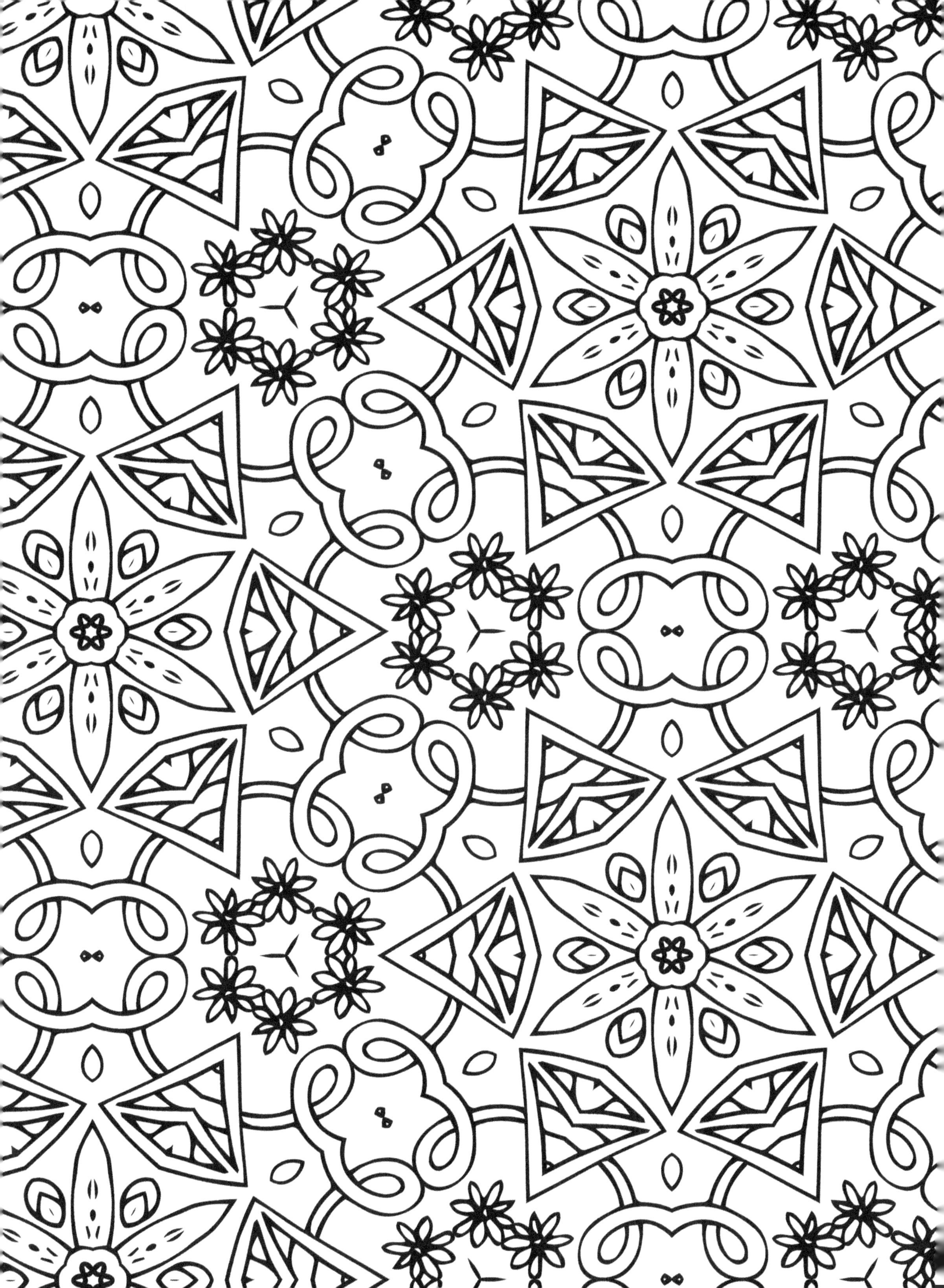

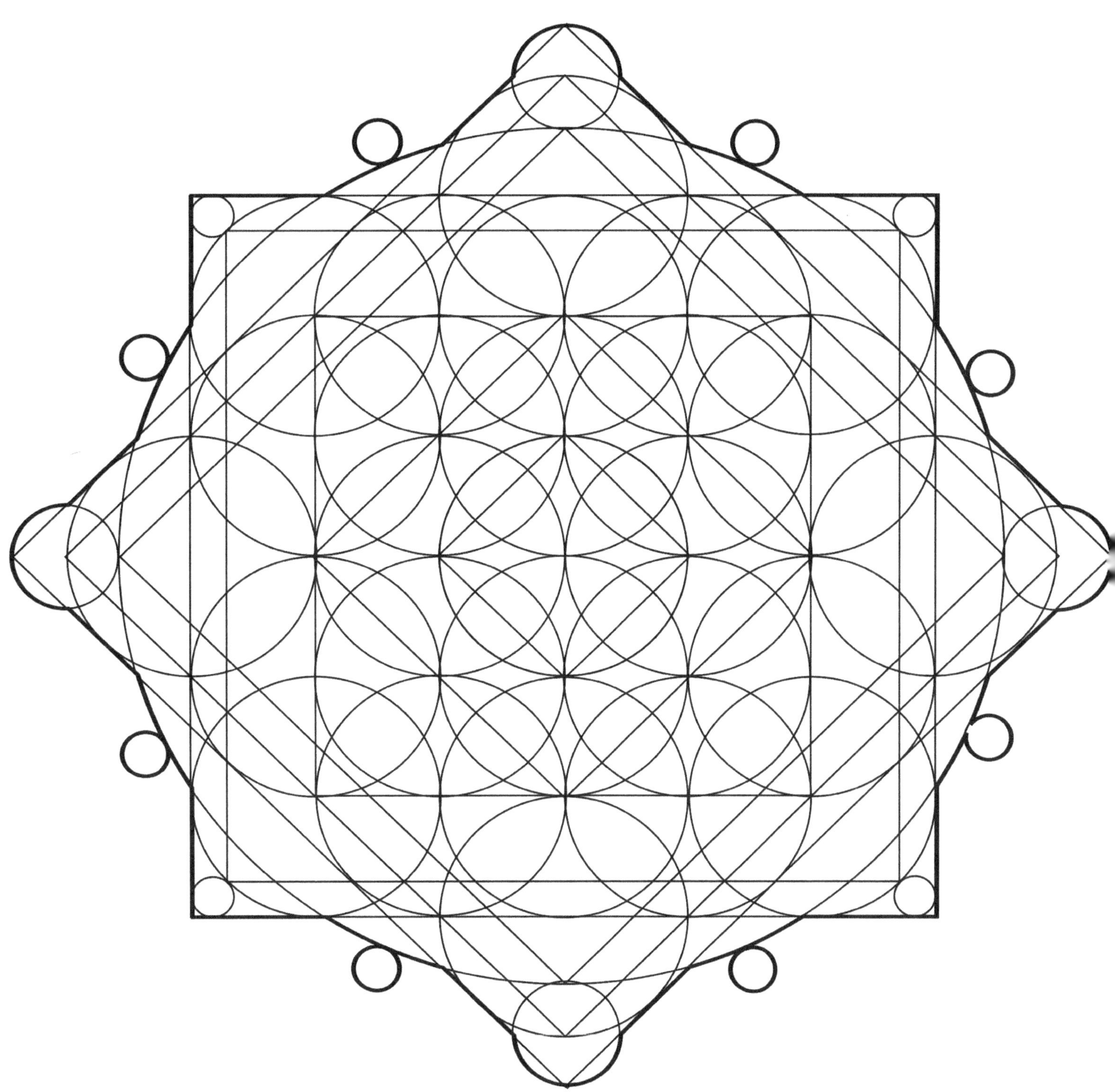

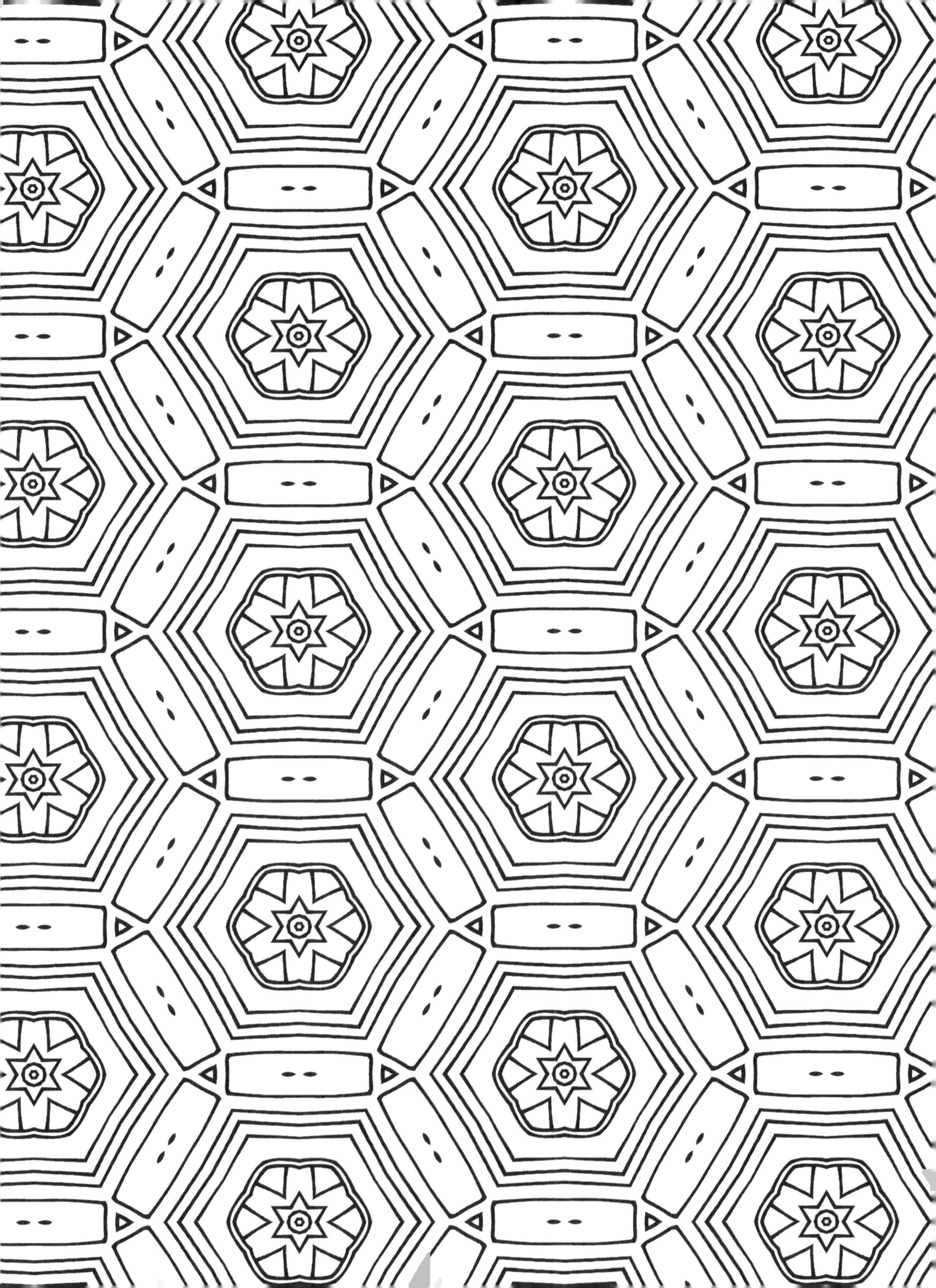

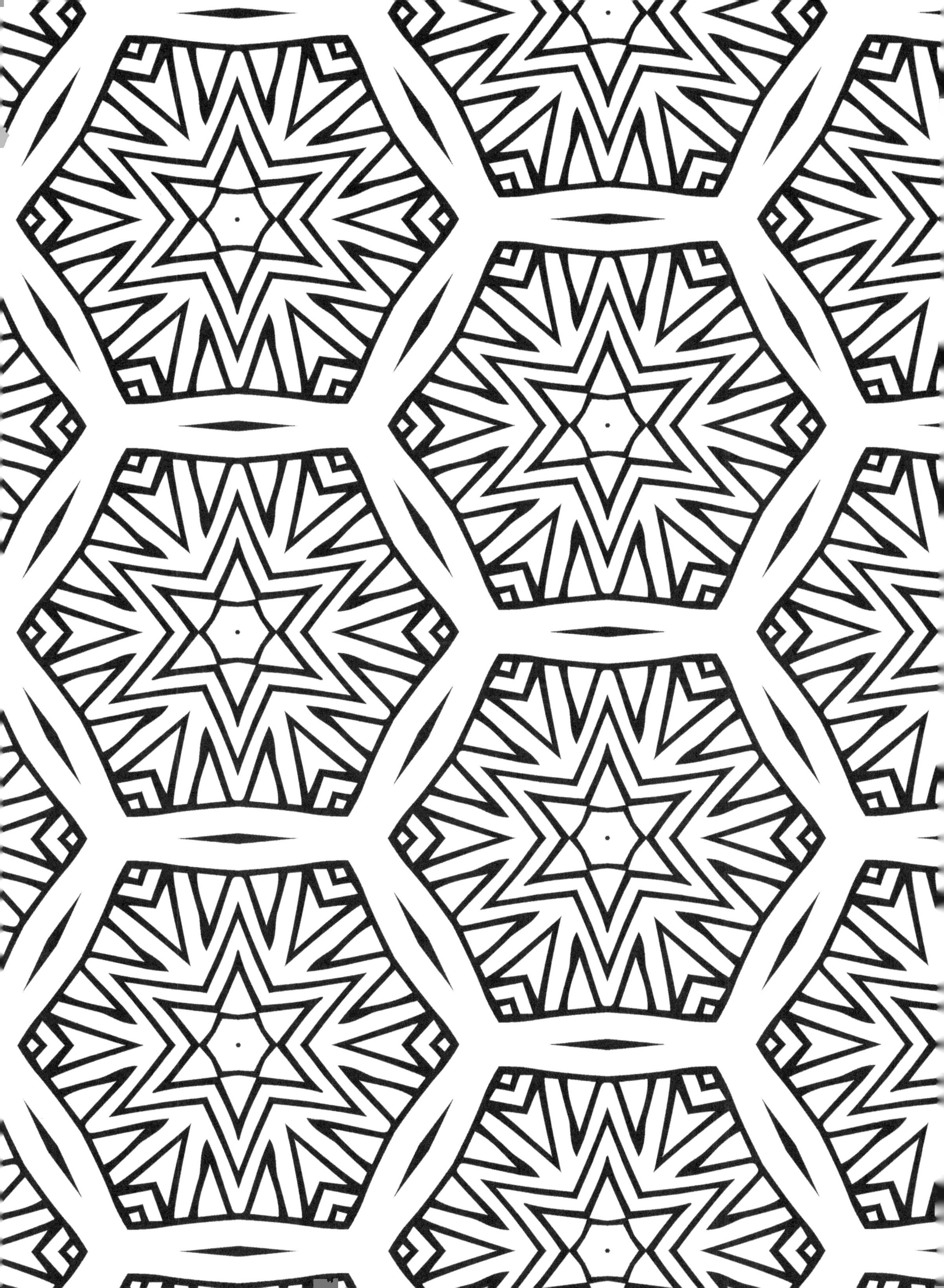

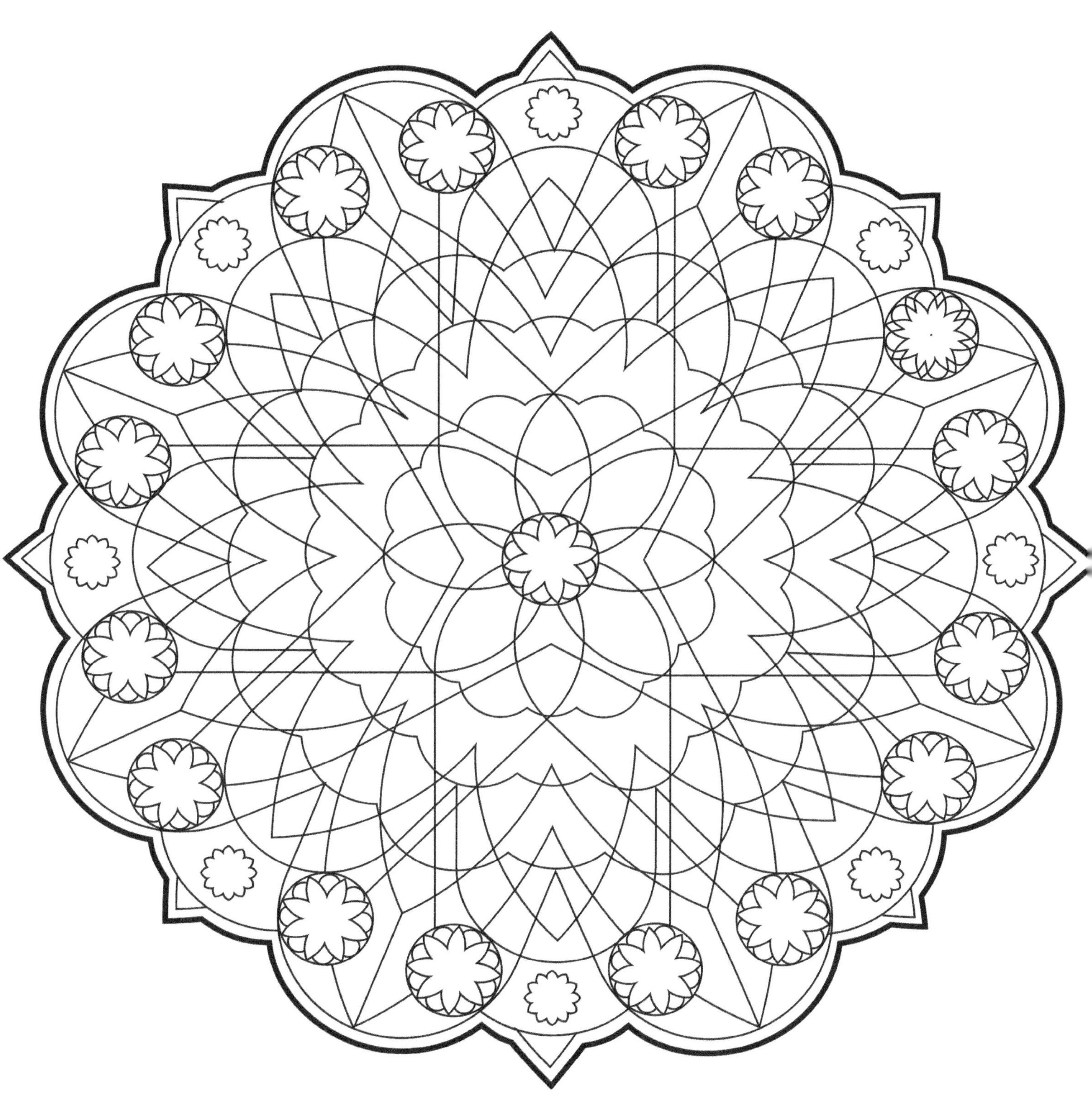

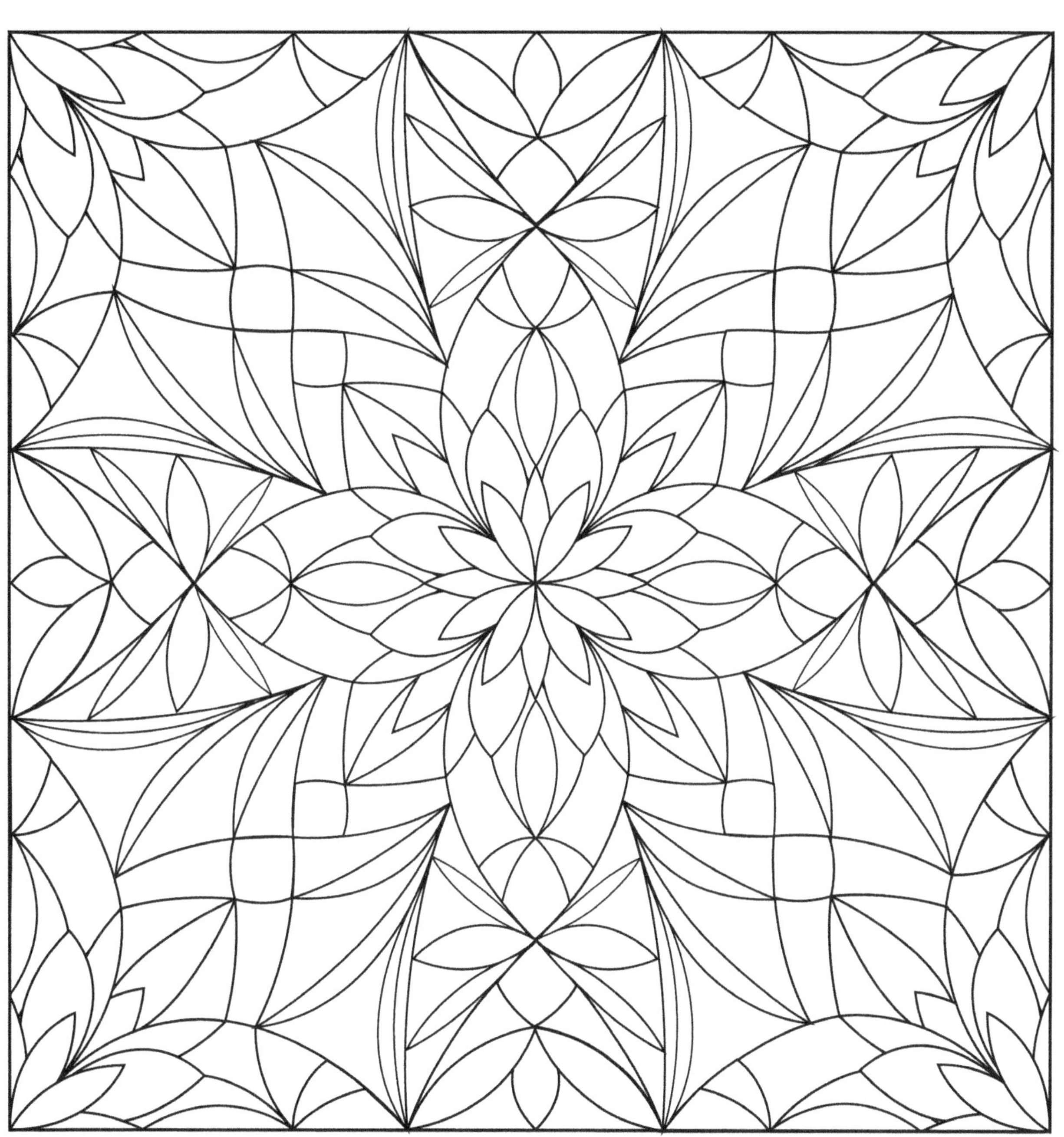

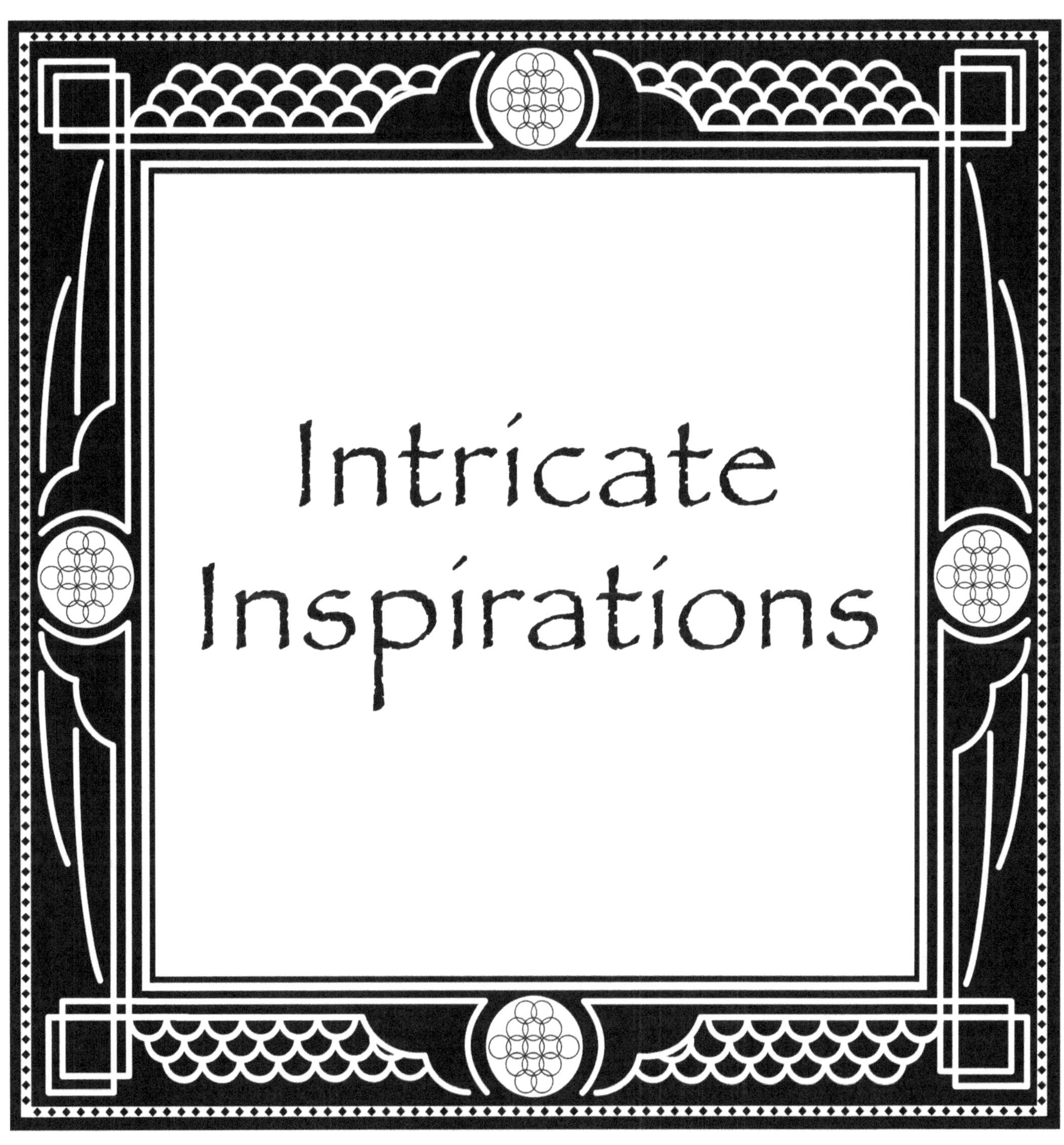

Intricate
Inspirations

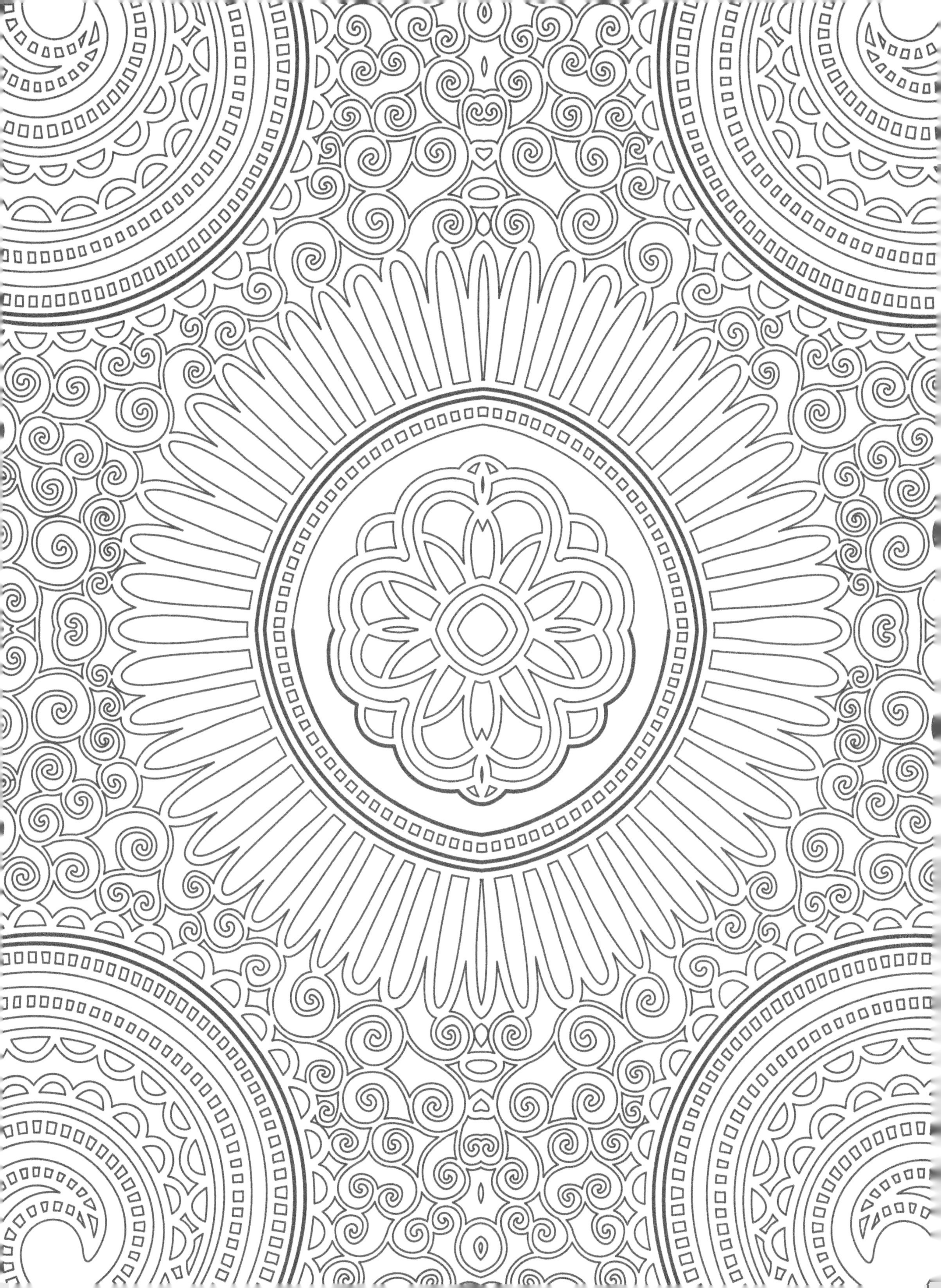

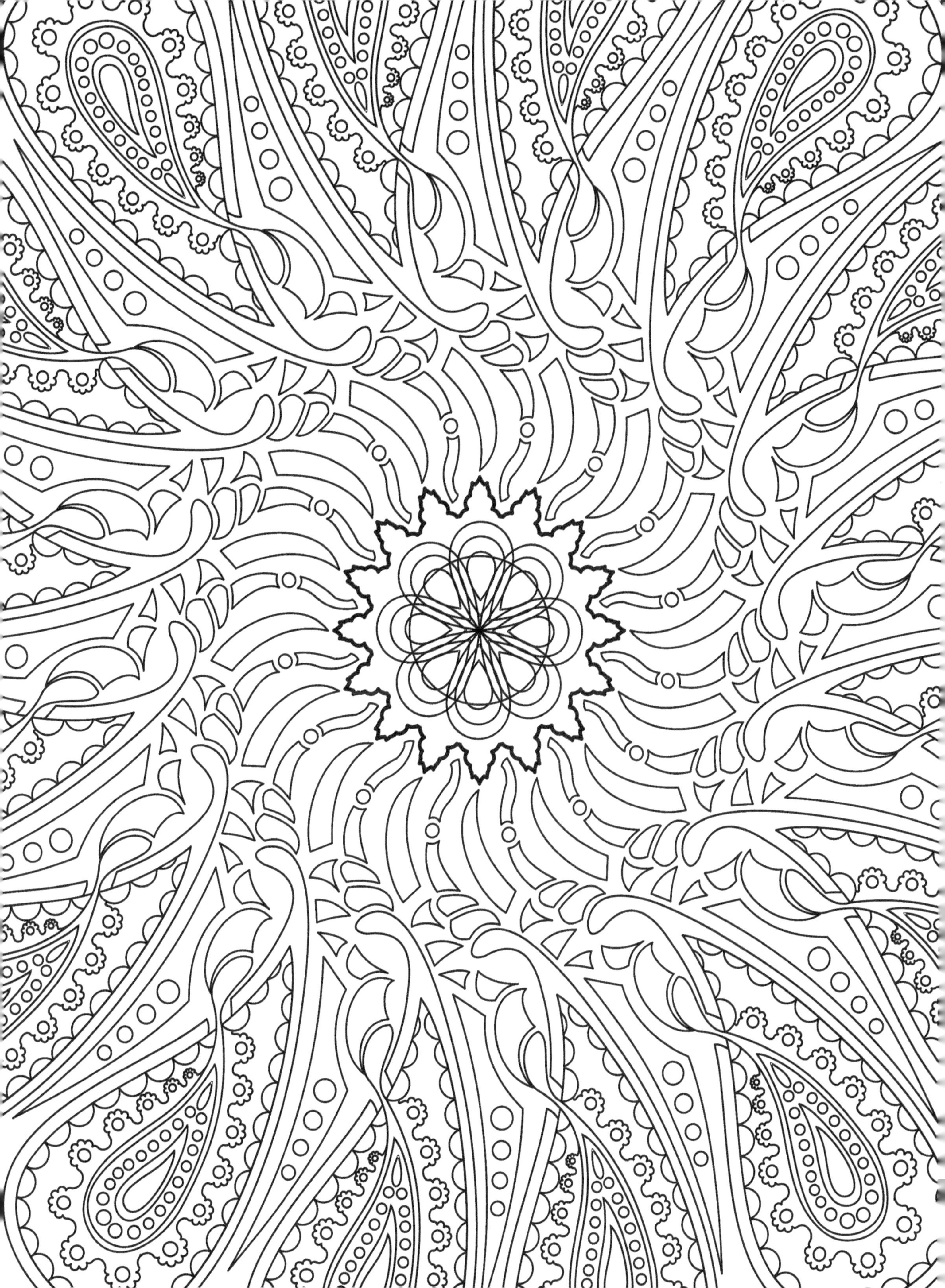

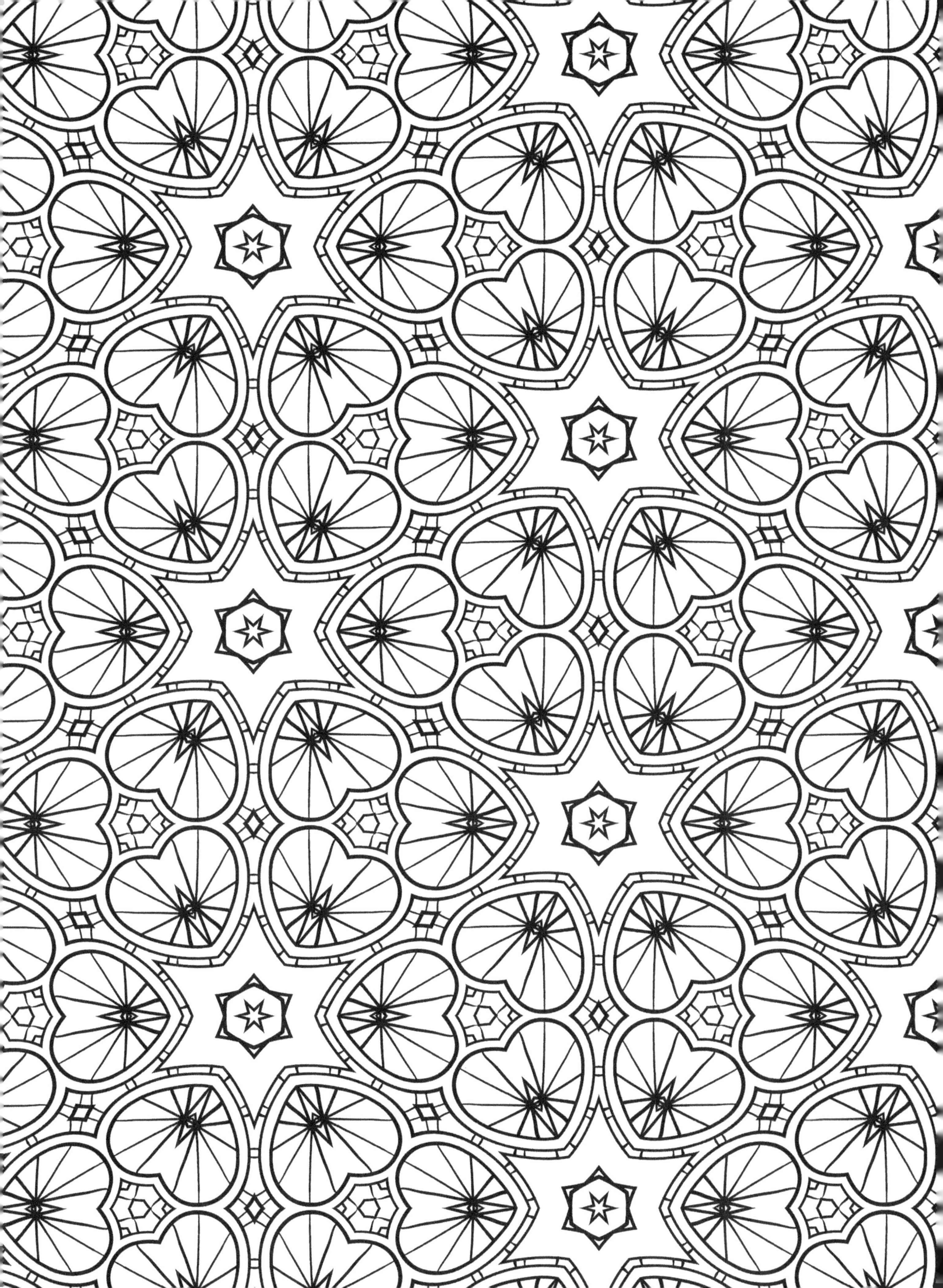

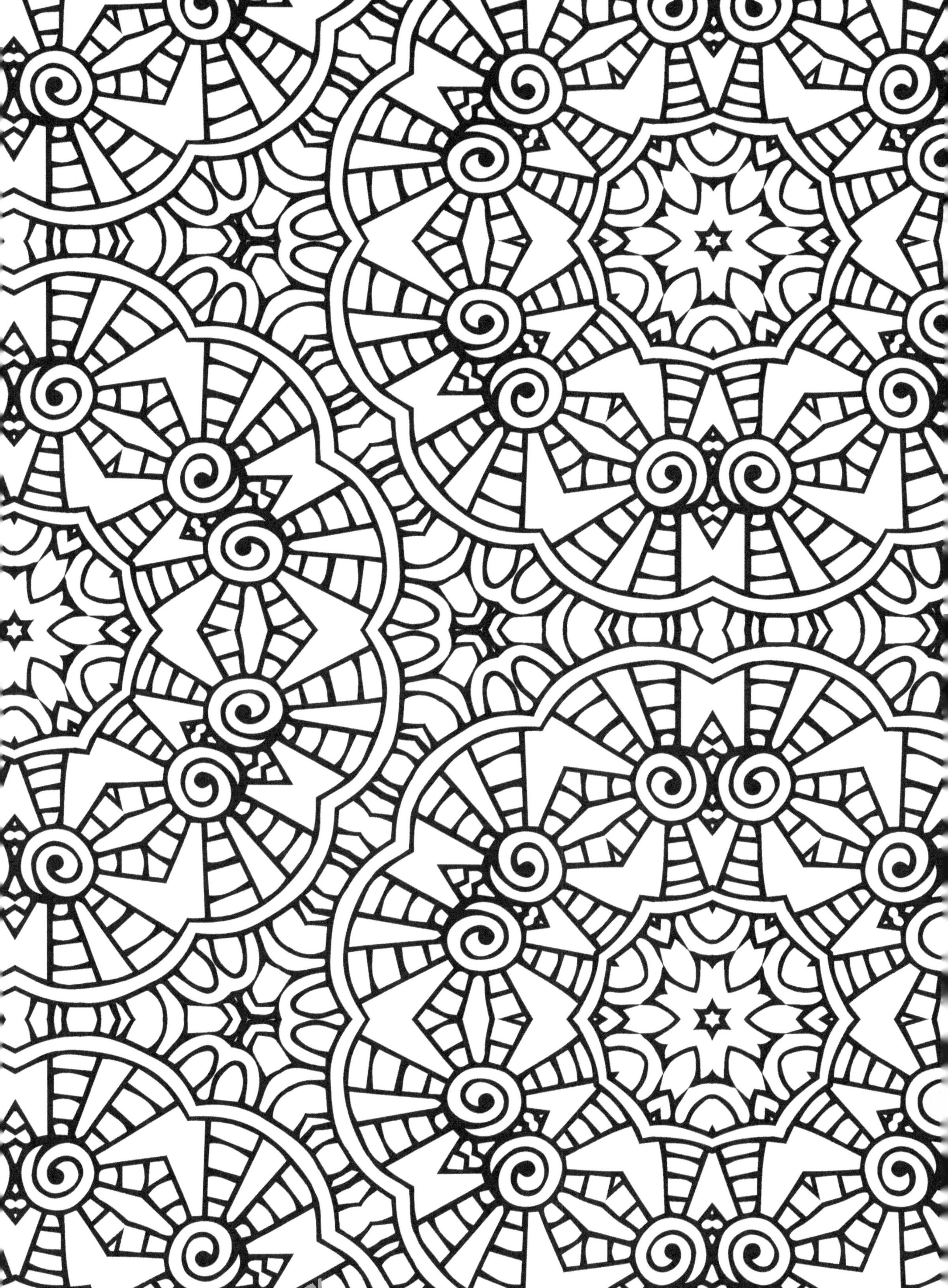

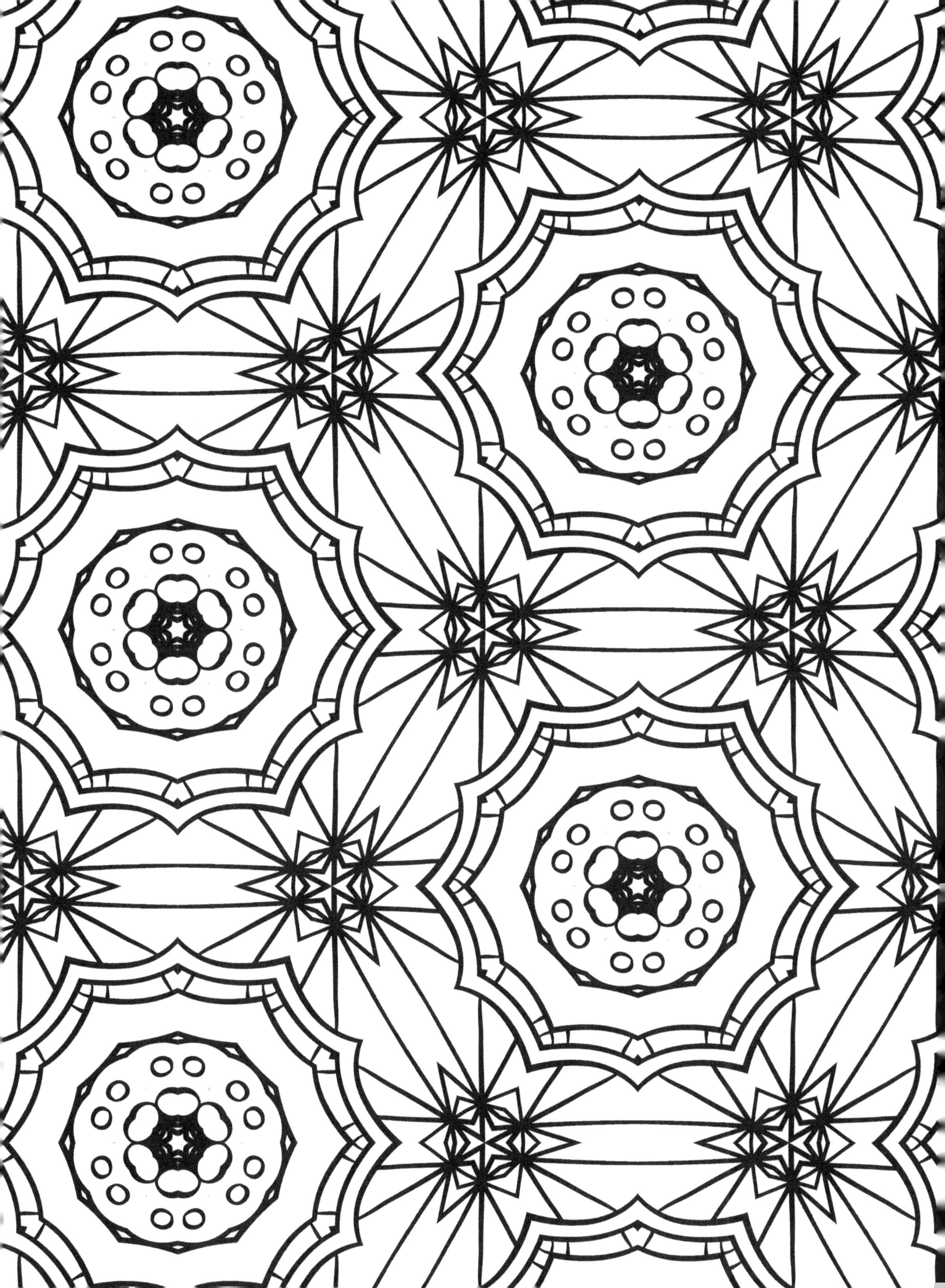

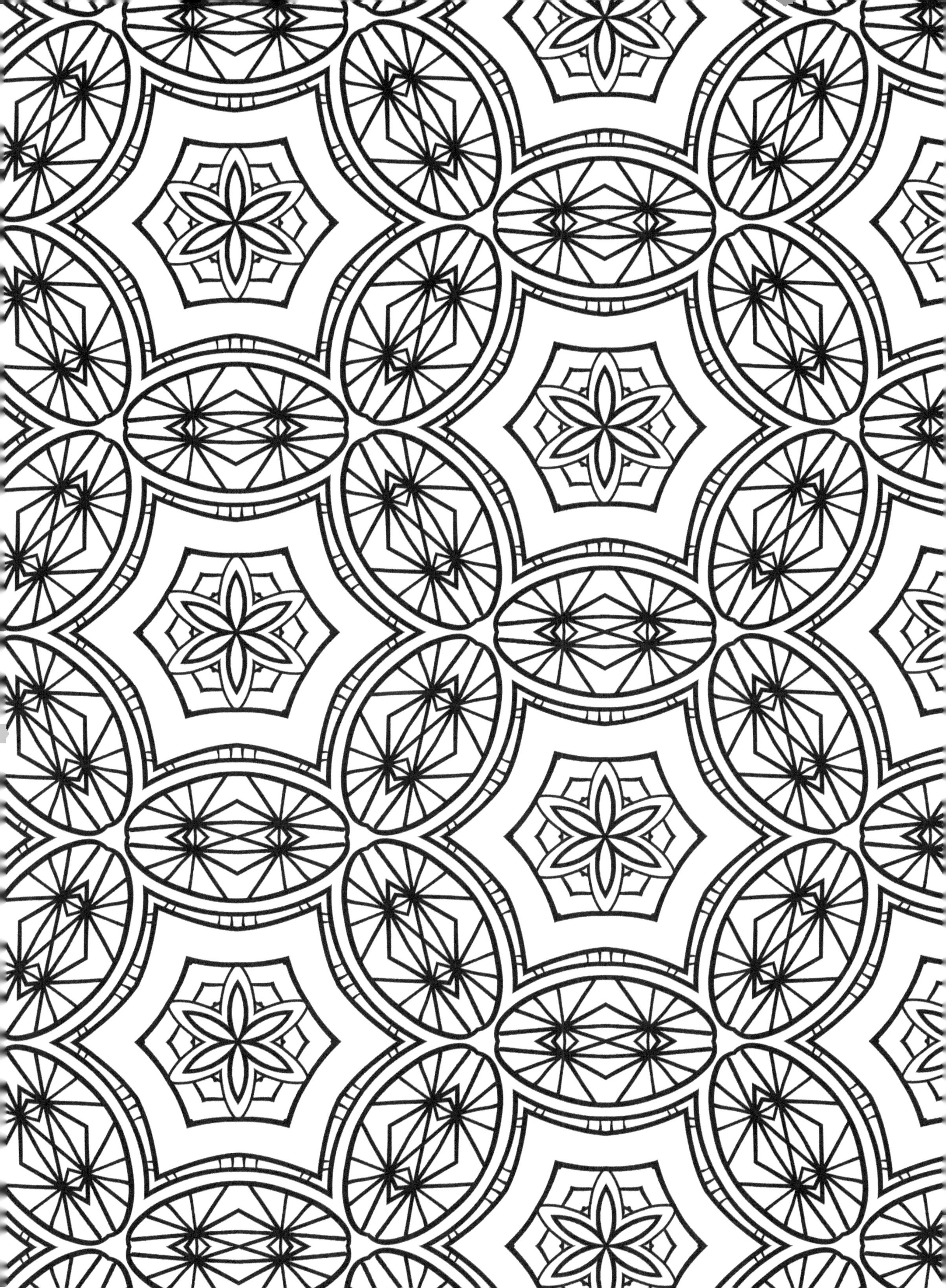

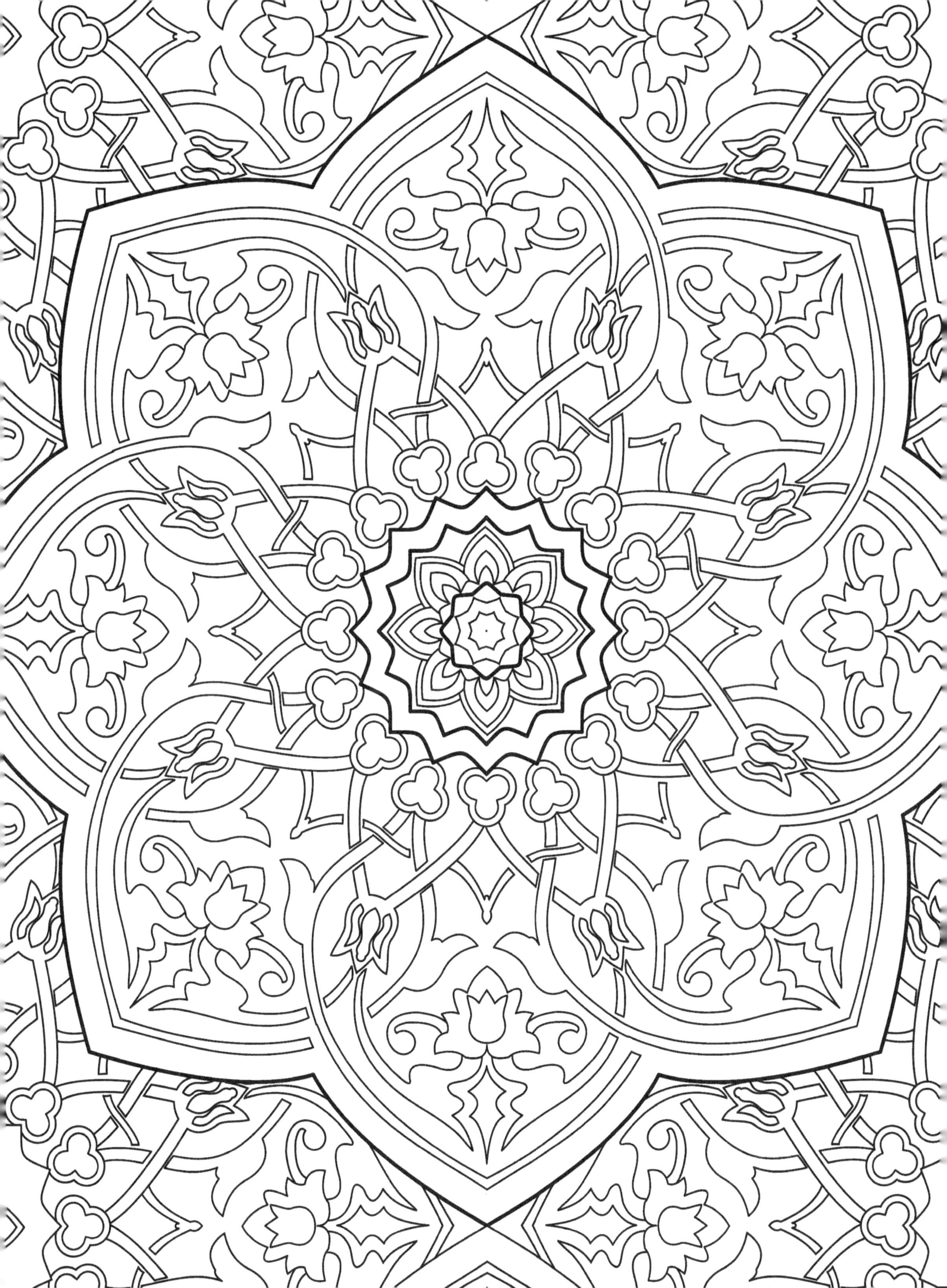

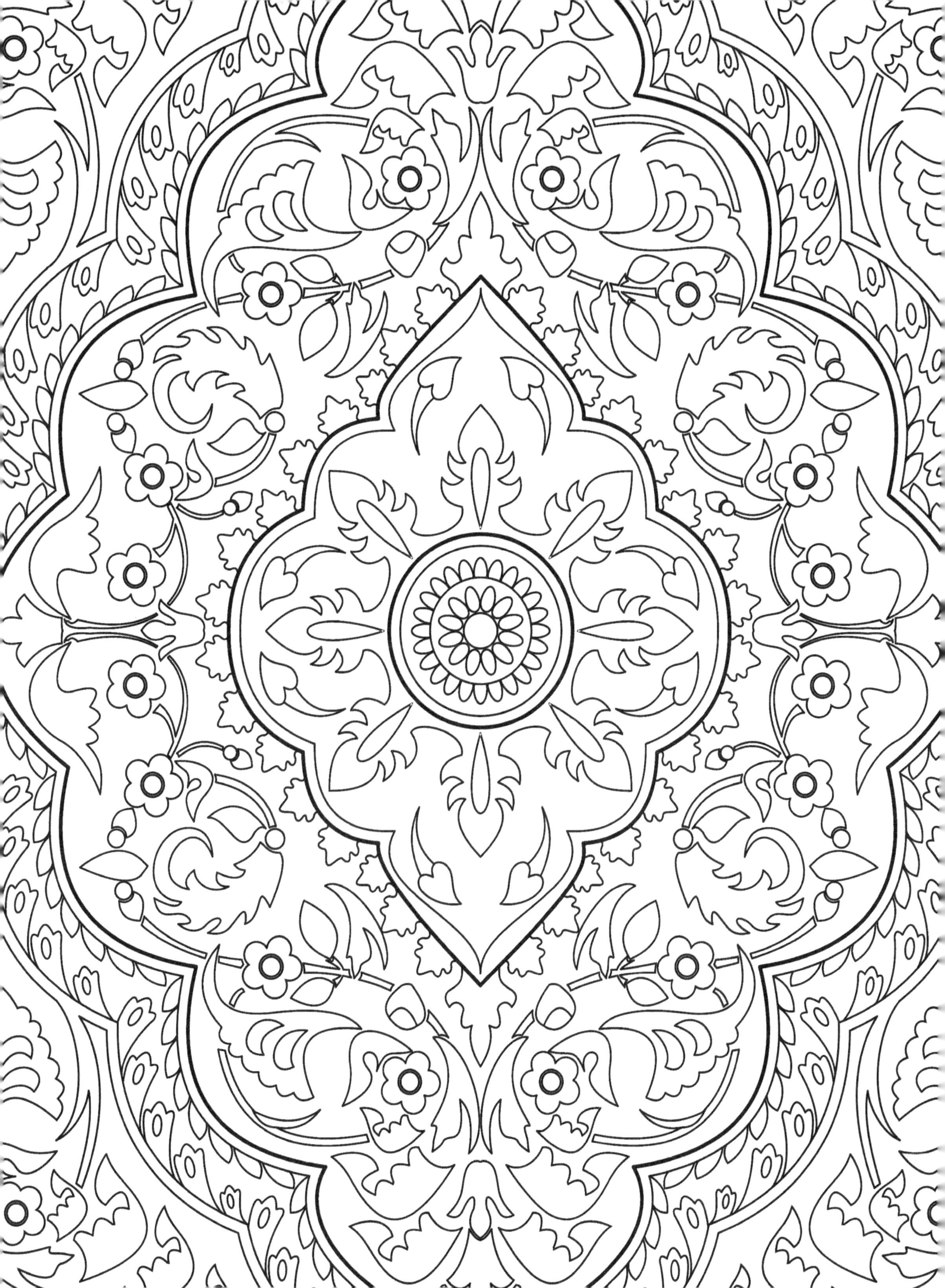

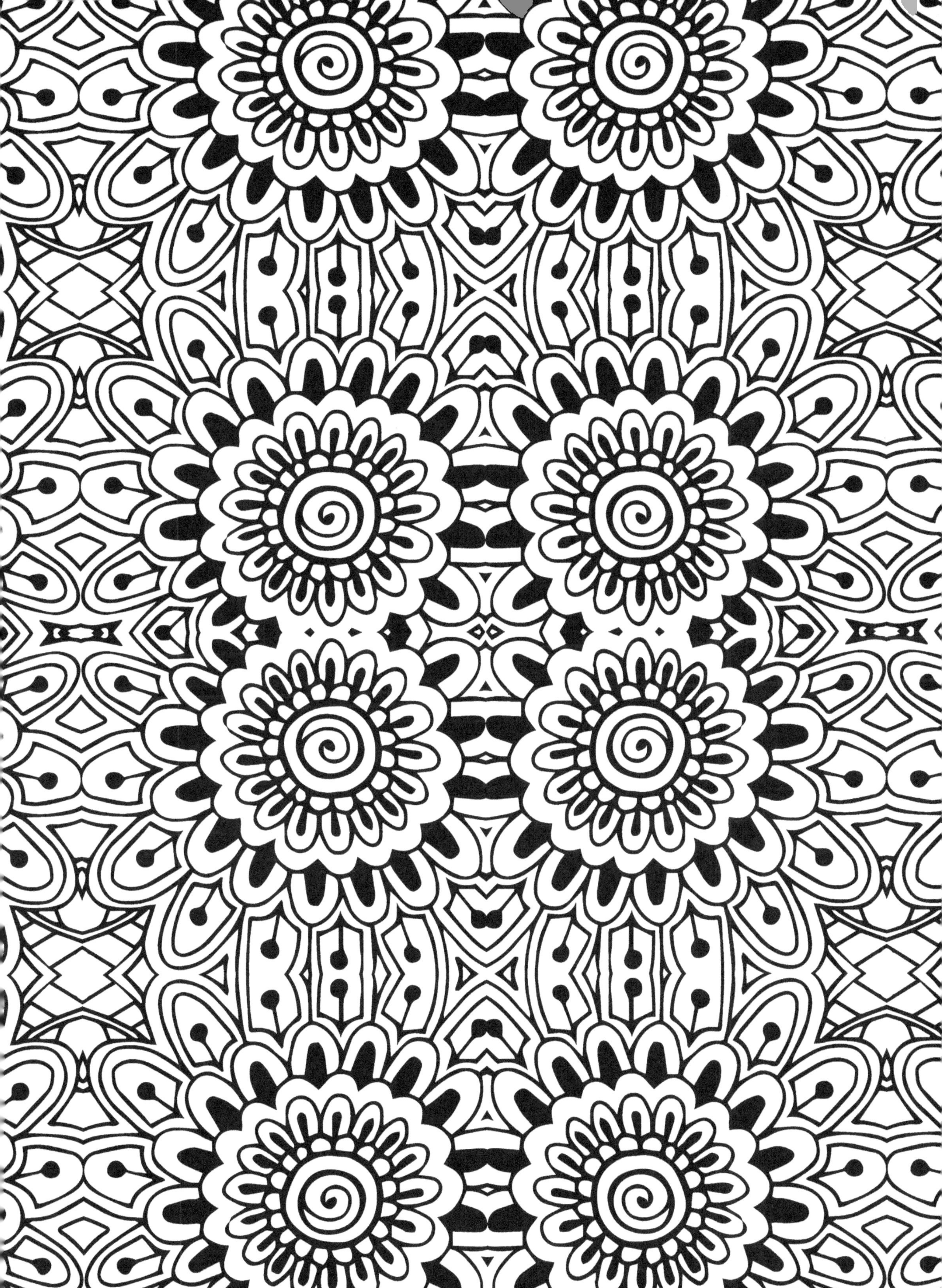

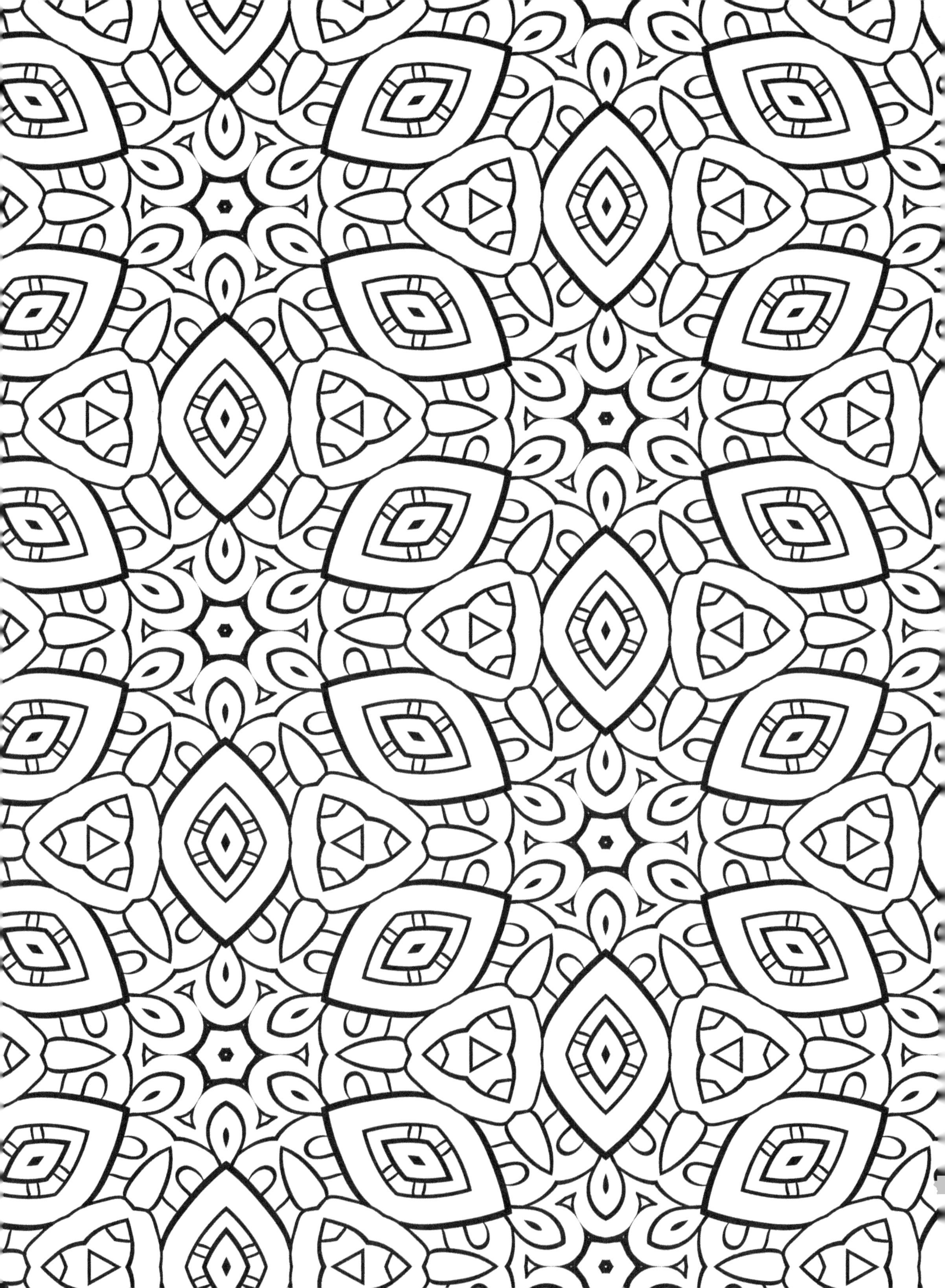

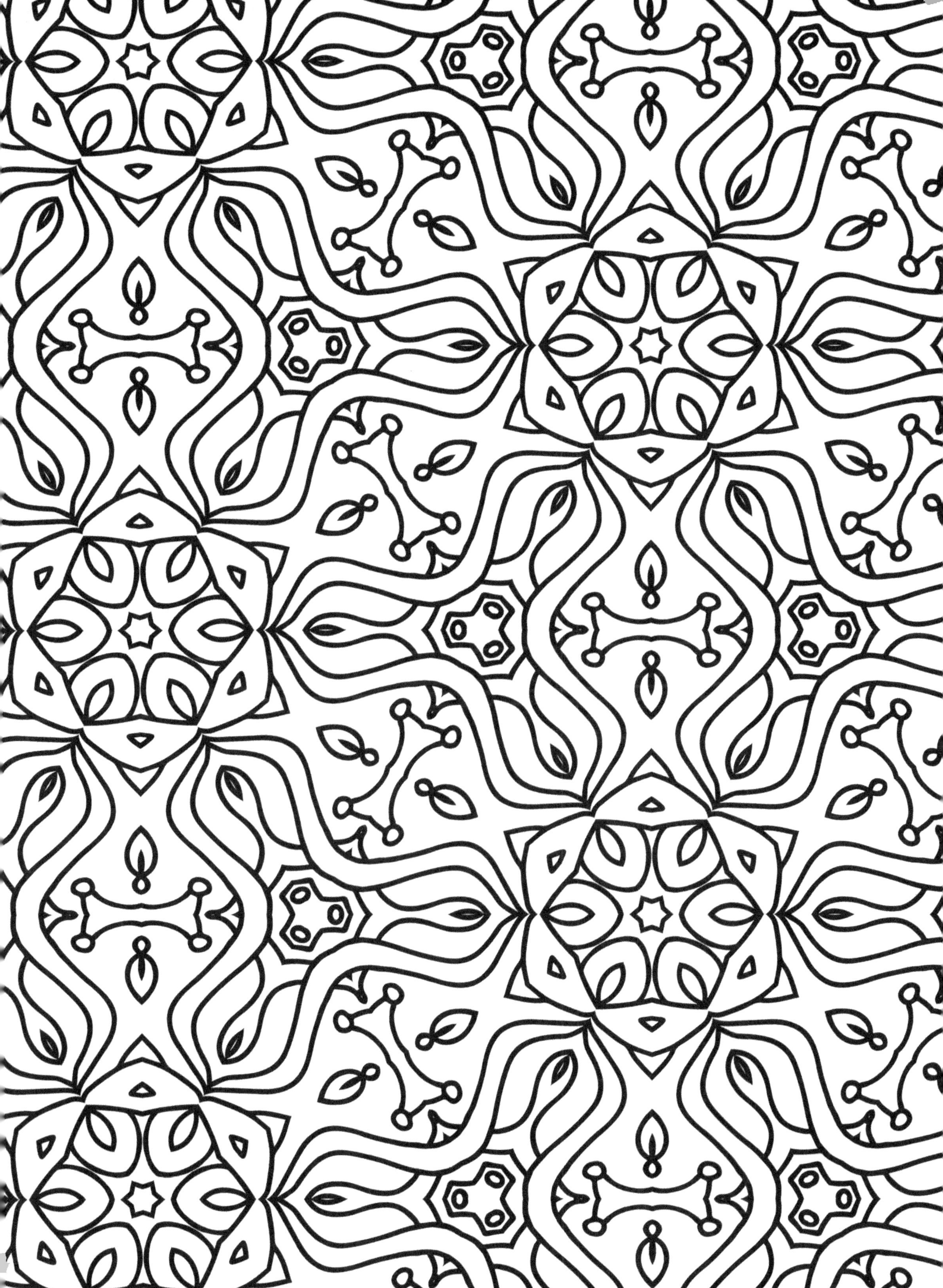

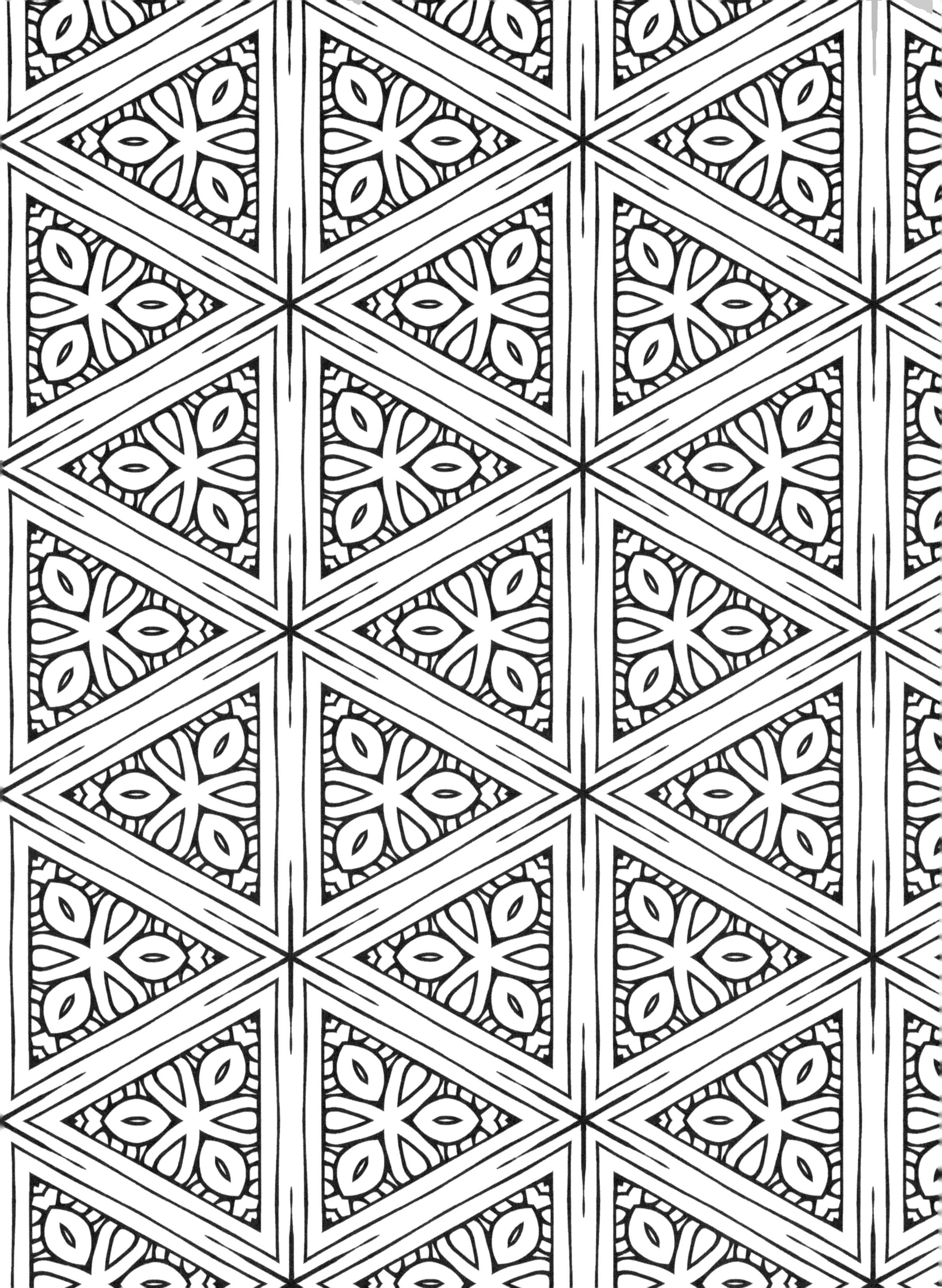

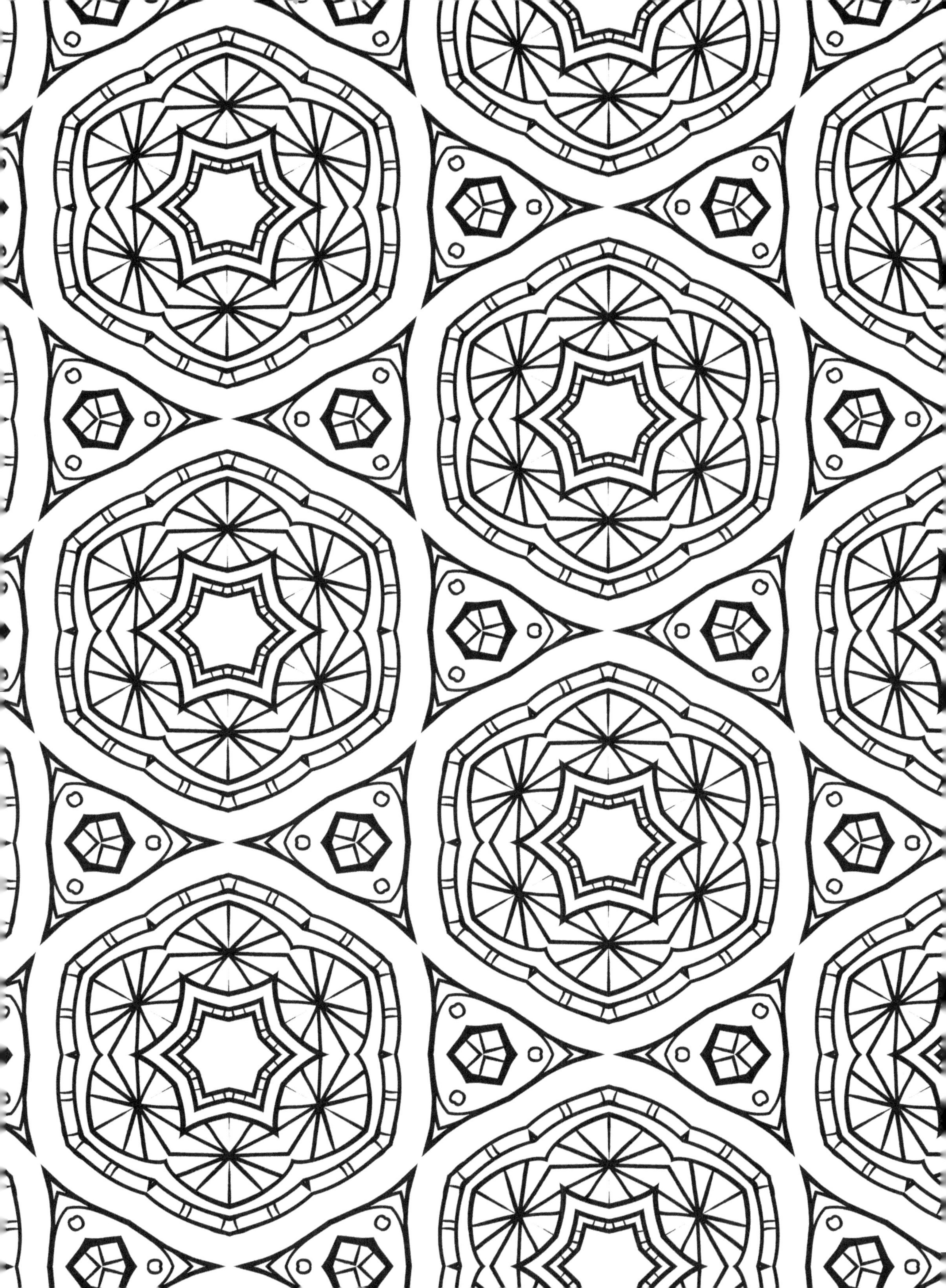

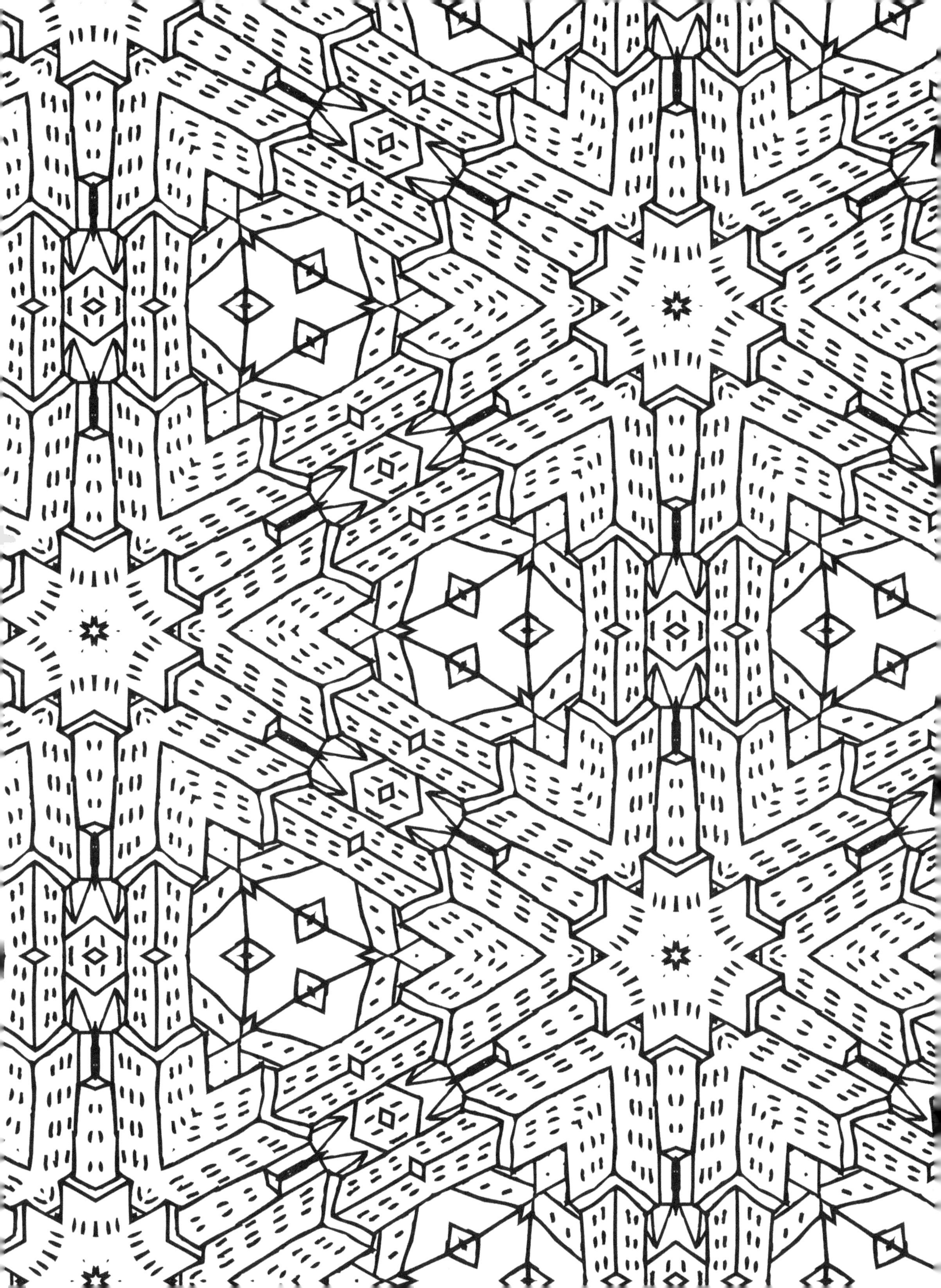

If you enjoyed colouring these designs, then move onto another book in the Progressive Patterns series of Adult Colouring Books.

We are sure you will love them!

We are amazed by the way that each of our designs looks so different when it has been coloured, so please share. We love to see your finished designs, don't be shy, head over to our Facebook page and show us what you have created.

https://www.facebook.com/progressivepatternsadultcolouringbooks

Look out for our other colouring books created by nikk nakk designs.

- Simple Styles
- Decorative Designs
- Intricate Inspirations
- Progressive Patterns Volume 1
- Progressive Patterns - A Man's World
- Progressive Patterns for Lefties
- Fairies and Flowers

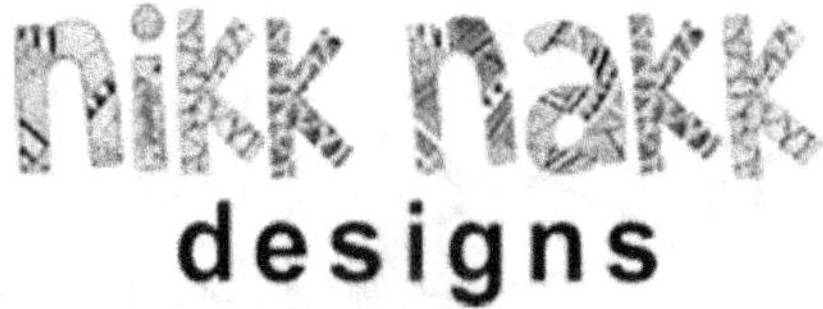